The
HUSBAND'S
Cookbook

The Kitchen Sink Papers:
My Life as a Househusband

The

HUSBAND'S

Cookbook

Mike McGrady

J. B. Lippincott Company

NEW YORK

U.S. Library of Congress Cataloging in Publication Data

McGrady, Mike.
    The husband's cookbook.

    Includes index.
    1. - Cookery.   I. - Title.
TX652.M2247   641.5   79–15722
ISBN–0–397–01372–8

80 81 82 83 10 9 8 7 6 5 4 3

CONTENTS

This book is dedicated to the woman who, by general agreement, is the finest cook of them all. I refer of course to

GRACE ROBINSON McGRADY,

who, strictly by coincidence, is my mom.

PREFACE

Not too long ago my wife and I traded roles for a year. Every morning she went off to an office and earned the money that paid the bills. I stayed at home, cooked and cleaned, picked up after three kids, went head-to-head with bargain-hunting shoppers, pleaded for a raise in allowance, and lived the generally hellish life that half the human race accepts as its lot. I lived to tell that story in a book called *The Kitchen Sink Papers: My Life as a Househusband.*

There's much about that year I'd just as soon forget. Ironing, for example. Matching up socks. Pasting trading stamps into little booklets. Or just simple house cleaning. Any job that requires six hours to do and can be undone in six minutes by one small child carrying a plate of crackers and a Monopoly set is not a job that will long hold my interest. My current thinking on the matter: If the debris accumulates to a point where small animals can be seen to be living there, it should be cleaned up, preferably by someone hired for the occasion.

The only part of the job I truly enjoyed was the cooking, and that's something I still enjoy. Cooking is the only part of keeping a home that demands creativity. When you dust a table, there is no need to dust that table a different way each time out. However, every meal presents a different set of problems and solutions. Then, too, there is no sure way to judge success or failure with most aspects of keeping a home, but with cooking the reaction is instantaneous and difficult to disguise.

It's surprising to me that more husbands haven't taken over at least some of the cooking. It beats most of the traditional husbandly chores; it's a hell of a lot more fun than raking leaves. Moreover, at one time, most men do at least some cooking. During that expanse of time separating life with mom from life with wife, it's either cook or perish.

Twenty years ago and more, during my bachelor days, I fancied myself as something of a chef. I had developed and perfected a spaghetti sauce that has not been altered significantly since then. (You'll see it in Menu 1.) And back then, in my early twenties, I learned to put together a hamburger that will still lend luster to any luncheon. (See Menu 19.)

Bachelors soon learn that knowing how to cook can be as much of a romantic plus as knowing how to wear tuxedos or when to buy long-stemmed roses. This is the simple truth of the matter: The shortest distance to *anyone's* heart is through the stomach. When the man is doing the cooking, there is an added ingredient—novelty. Men, whether they be bachelors or husbands, will see few sights more memorable than the way a woman's eyes can soften in the flickering light cast by a duck flambé.

My repertoire, though impressive enough in some particulars, was laughably limited in range. In truth, it is quite possible that the reason I am married today is that I proposed quickly, before having run through the roster of eight dishes that I had thoroughly mastered.

During the months following marriage, that list expanded. Out of necessity. For there I was, suddenly married to a twenty-year-old girl who had been attending college, majoring in existential philosophy and Far Eastern religions. The cooking was up to me.

During that first year of marriage, there were formidable obstacles to culinary success. Money was a problem—actually, absence of money was the problem—so much of my culinary research was in the field of frankfurters. In this time of great nutritional ignorance, our diet was regularly supplemented with frozen dinners, pizza pie, and the like. Ketchup was not so much a condiment as a necessity, covering up a steady run of miscalculations. Somehow—relying on friends, on luck, on fast-food stands—we managed to get by.

Then my wife, Corinne, made what was to be a major error in judgment. One evening she volunteered to cook a meal all by herself. She said she wanted to experiment with a dish blending lamb shanks, sweet potatoes, green beans, and lemon juice. With just a touch of condescension, and perhaps more than a touch of skepticism, I agreed to let her try.

How well did she do? Well, you can determine this for yourself when you get to Menu 17. I can best describe the quality of that meal by pointing out, simply, that it would be fifteen years before another meal would be prepared under my personal direction.

What happened was not all that unusual—was, in fact, the very opposite of unusual. We just stepped into our proper roles, our expected roles, and began reading our lines from scripts written through many generations. The roles? Male and Female. It was my job to make the living—first by writing books for children, then slick magazine stories, and finally a newspaper column. Corinne played Female. That is to say, she gave birth to three children and thereafter shared their world; in her spare time she did the budget-balancing and the cleaning and the cooking.

In retrospect, it's slightly incredible that she did it all so routinely and without complaint. She did it because it was expected, because it was what all the women in her family did and what all the women in our world did. And since she was a young woman of intelligence and talent, she sought to apply her full range of skills to this new life.

There was no longer any need for me to waste my increasingly valuable time cooking. Besides, Corinne was so good at that. There was even something intimidating about competing with someone that accomplished. My course of action was an obvious one. I stopped cooking.

And this is the way life went on for many years, the way life would have always gone on except for the discovery of something known as Women's Liberation. One day, as a direct result of this discovery, our faithful housekeeper and family cook went out on strike. Fortunately, by this time the three children were fairly well launched in life and starvation was not a genuine threat to any of us.

In our home, and in other homes not unlike ours, we witnessed the Big Change. Houses that had always been spotless were now considerably less than that. Children who had grown up in the constant company of a nursey-cook-chauffeur were being left to their own devices. The dinner tables in our neighborhood, and maybe in yours, became deprived areas.

Well, when slavery was abolished, the plantation owners had to do some of the work themselves. After this most recent emancipation, it was clearly my responsibility to take up some of the slack. But which slack? And how? One meets the most pressing needs first. Since I had once been able to cook, that would surely present no major problems. Except, in the passing of time, I had lost all interest in cooking and my old recipes had lost much of their magic. Most of my original recipes called for ketchup or a healthy shot of A.1. Sauce as a primary ingredient; I knew better than that now, but after a full day in an office and an hour on a crowded highway, anything more elaborate seemed out of the question. Consequently, I did what a whole generation of American males was doing; I learned the shortest routes to McDonald's and to Kentucky Fried Chicken stands.

Fast food, however, fails as a way of life, and before much longer I began relearning how to cook. Not without my share of disasters. My first attempt at a chocolate mousse produced a green and gluey substance. As it turned out, I am the only man ever to construct something out of chocolate that my children refused to eat.

Nor am I able to forget my first soufflé. Of course I had heard other cooks describe some of the perils of soufflé making. And so, to guarantee success, I decided to make Julia Child's "noncollapsible soufflé." This turned out to be the greatest misnomer since someone named a ship *Titanic*. Not only did the soufflé refuse to rise, it seemed to want to hide, sinking ever deeper into the pan as if cowering in its own shame. It was a leaden, soggy pancake of eggs, cheese, and mushrooms, your basic complete culinary disaster.

But this, too, is part of cooking, and one must learn to be philosophical about the catastrophes. I can now accept the fact that in every cook's life an occasional soufflé must fall. And in time the successes tended to outnumber the failures.

I took to reading cookbooks with the kind of avidity that I previously reserved for a John Cheever novel. And I quickly saw that there was no reason to settle for a simple pork chop when an herbed pork chop was no more difficult. The only real difference between scrambled eggs and an omelet *aux fines herbes* is a few minutes of practice.

I discovered there was an abundance of assistance available to the starting cook. I began learning with the primers, *The Joy of Cooking* and Fanny Farmer. The year I traded places with my wife I began to rely on the cookbooks of Craig Claiborne the way I would rely on any true friend in my hour of need. I found Craig to be reliable and uncomplicated, two virtues that have always enhanced friendships. It was then that I discovered James Beard and his cookbooks. For a while there, James Beard became my main man, and more recently, as I've gotten into wok cookery and meatless meals, I've learned a great deal from the excellent vegetarian cookbooks of Anna Thomas.

Most cooks learn most of their cooking from their family, and I'm no exception. I come from a long line of fine cooks, all female. Many of my recipes have been handed down from my grandmother, Elizabeth Robinson. Much of the information, not to mention the inspiration, has come from my mom, Grace, who is, by general agreement, the finest cook in the world. I've learned a lot from them and from my wife and from my Aunt Frances and from my Cousin Jo, who thought to collect the best of the family recipes in a book long before the notion ever crossed my mind.

It was something of a surprise to learn that a cookbook is something that can be read and used by men as well as by women. Strange as it may seem, not all women want their husbands to know this fact. As often as not, the same women who berate their husbands for not doing their fair share around the house will become even more critical when those same husbands pitch in and start to whip up a little dinner for the family.

I'm always surprised when I hear a woman disparaging a husband's first tentative gestures toward actually cooking a meal. I've seen wives taste a husband's first attempt and give out with one of those condescending compliments: "It's okay, but the next time you might want to add a little salt." And I've been flat-out astonished when a husband's culinary offering is greeted by a complaint: "This kitchen is a *mess*! How come it takes you ten pots to make one little dish?"

I can only conclude that many women don't want their

husbands to know how easy it is—or how much fun it can be—to cook a meal. The truth is this: It is perfectly possible for a person of either sex to walk into a kitchen the first time out and make a perfectly acceptable dinner for the family. Why don't all women want this information broadcast widely? Perhaps it's because some women still don't realize that it's just as easy, and maybe even just as much fun, to go out into the business world and do those mysterious things that their husbands do all day long.

The prospect of reversing roles is threatening to us all. When we have finally solved the problems attached to being a man or a woman, when we have repeated those solutions over and over again until we are comfortable with them, it's not easy to take on a whole new set of problems. And so we let George do it. Or we let Georgina do it.

It may seem absurd to view the preparation of food as a sex-linked characteristic. But whenever we first cross over one of those invisible barriers separating the traditional male and female roles, everyone is threatened. I can remember, as I first took over the full cooking chores for the family, I was hoping against hope that none of my more macho pals would hear about it.

At my neighborhood saloon, for example, I had never bothered to mention my cooking prowess. I would talk about the latest baseball results or a recent horse race and even, on rare occasions, a current book. But I never ever sought to trade recipes with the others who inhabit the same gin mill. Except on one occasion.

Linda, the strikingly beautiful young barmaid there, had only one weakness that the regulars were ever able to see. Through those long afternoons and evenings, surrounded by grizzled old men attempting to remain upright, Linda would take slices of fresh tomato, dip them into a small jar of mayonnaise, and then pop them into her mouth. During a typical eight-hour shift, Linda would munch her way through half a dozen tomatoes and a great quantity of mayonnaise. It was, as I said, her only apparent weakness.

"You know something?" I told her one day. "You really ought to make your own mayonnaise. There's nothing to it."

"Are you kidding? I can't even boil water."

"You don't have to boil water," I said. "You don't have to boil anything. Look, I'll bring you in some of mine."

"Yours? You mean your wife's, don't you?"

"No, mine." Here I lowered my voice. "I've been doing all the cooking at home. I'll bring you in some homemade mayonnaise tomorrow. You'll see."

"I won't hold my breath."

"You'll see."

"Sure."

So young and so skeptical. Well, Linda had heard many offers in her time, the full line of propositions, but this was the first time a customer ever offered to bring her some homemade mayonnaise. The next day at noon, when I showed up with a small container of fresh-made mayonnaise, I was rewarded by an expression of surprise that came close to out-and-out shock. This was replaced, as she tasted the mayonnaise, by an expression that bordered on the beatific.

"Did you ever consider leaving your family?" she asked. Before I could give adequate consideration to this offer, Linda made a public announcement to the other regulars at the bar. "Hey, everyone, you've got to try this mayo. Mike made it himself."

"What're you tryna tell us?" a white-haired customer said. "You tryna tell us you can make mayonnaise at home?"

"Sure, there's nothing to it."

To say that the mayonnaise was well received is to understate the case. Before the afternoon was out, I had to print the recipe on half a dozen cocktail napkins. Who knows whether anyone there ever actually went to the trouble of making mayonnaise? But this I do know: At that moment, with a bunch of unshaven men asking me for my recipe for mayonnaise, I stopped worrying about what the rest of the world might think about my role as a cook. You'll find that mayo recipe, incidentally, in Menu 16.

Now just a word to those of you who are approaching the kitchen for the first time.

You'll find that the first recipes in this book are the easiest ones and the last ones are the most difficult. Although all are well within the range of the unpracticed cook, it might be best to begin at the beginning and end at the end.

But don't let any of the recipes scare you off. If you're not intimidated, you'll soon find out just how much fun cooking can be. Although all these meals will please the most discriminating of palates, they're all easy. This is, after all, a cookbook written for husbands, especially those husbands who don't know for sure which switch turns on which burner. It's for all of you who have never quite managed to find your way beyond the refrigerator to the stove.

We're going to begin with the simplest meal of them all, spaghetti, but by the end of the book we'll be cooking Chicken Kiev together. (You gotta believe!) By the time you've worked your way through these fifty-two complete meals, you'll have completed a basic course in cookery and you should be able to improvise any number of dishes.

Each of the sections will begin with a checklist of the staples that should already be on hand—flour, salt, pepper, sugar, and so forth. Make sure they *are* on hand. If not, add them to the detailed shopping list that follows. I'll be telling you exactly what you'll have to buy at the supermarket before beginning the cooking. I say *you* because as long as you're doing the cooking, you should do the shopping as well. If this accomplishes nothing else, it'll help you understand where all that money goes every week.

With each recipe, a schedule is provided, a minute-by-minute timetable showing how much time is required for both the preparation and the cooking. This rough schedule will enable even the most neophytic of cooks to serve dinner promptly at 6:30 PM. (No? Well, would you believe 7:30?)

You'll find the cooking instructions are written as simply as possible. I find that what makes cooking fun is the casual approach, flexibility. If you feel like experimenting, do it. I also find that what makes cooking difficult is rigidity, trying to figure out the difference between a third of a teaspoon and three eighths of a teaspoon. Here we'll always go for a more relaxed kind of cooking. Here it will be a "pinch" and a "dash" and a "handful" and, every now and then . . . a small prayer.

MENU 1

Spaghetti in Meat Sauce
Tossed Greens
Chianti
Brie Cheese and Crackers

We begin with spaghetti because it is easy, because it allows for improvisation, because it is easy, because everyone likes it, and, above all else, because it is easy.

The Staples: Make sure that these are on hand: salt, pepper, basil, oregano, thyme, butter, olive oil, garlic, vinegar.

The Shopping List: One pound of spaghetti, one pound ground beef, one large can Italian plum tomatoes, one small can tomato paste, crackers, Chianti wine. And these vegetables: two large onions, two green peppers, one bunch celery, one head lettuce, and half a pound of mushrooms. Also, two cheeses—half a pound of Parmesan and half a pound of Brie. This should be enough for a family of five.

4 PM: This first day we start early, allowing time to recover from small disasters along the way. An adequate spaghetti sauce can be prepared in less than an hour, but today's extra simmering time will only improve it.

Put half a stick of butter and a splash of olive oil into a

25

large saucepan over medium heat. When the butter has melted, add most of the thinly sliced onions and green peppers. (Save some of each for your salad.) Slice two celery stalks and add them. Peel and mince two cloves of garlic and sprinkle over the mixture. (*Danger!* A clove of garlic is not to be confused with the large bulb of garlic. Not ever.)

Stir with a wooden spoon. Other spoons may be used in an emergency, but wooden spoons will lend you a deceptively professional air. In a short time—ten minutes or so—the onions will turn golden brown at the edges. (*Danger!* If they turn golden black at the edges, turn down the heat at once.) Add the sliced mushrooms, cook for a few minutes, then turn off the heat.

4:25 PM: In a separate pan cook the ground beef over medium heat, breaking it into small chunks. When the meat is brown throughout, pour off the fat (*Danger!* Not in the sink!) and add the meat to the vegetables, again over medium heat.

4:40 PM: Stir in the canned tomatoes, the tomato paste, and the spices. The seasonings might include a large pinch of basil, another large pinch of oregano, a small pinch of thyme, and some salt and pepper. Trust your taste buds. Many other seasonings can be added—a bay leaf, a pinch of ground cloves, a few sprigs of parsley, some cayenne pepper. This is, in fact, a dish that invites experimentation. Any number of vegetables will enrich the sauce: eggplant, zucchini, chopped carrots—you name it. And should the sauce be too thick, it can be thinned with consommé, tomato juice, water, or wine.

When the sauce is well heated, reduce the heat to the lowest point, cover the pan, and allow the mixture to simmer gently. Stir the sauce occasionally. (*Danger!* If the mixture shows signs of sticking to the pot, the heat is too high.)

Take a little breather. Read the paper. Sample the Chianti. (One can't be too careful about these things.) Carry on a relaxed conversation with your wife, who is apt to be looking into the kitchen somewhat nervously.

5:40 PM: Start water boiling in the largest pot you can find.

6 PM: Make the spaghetti according to the box directions. While the water is boiling, you can put together the salad. Chop up a couple of stalks of celery and add that to the leftover slices of pepper and onion. Rinse the lettuce free of sand. Pat it dry with paper towels and break it into bite-sized pieces. The salad dressing, three parts oil and one part vinegar, is kept to the side until ready to serve.

6:15 PM: There are many ways to determine when the spaghetti is ready. In ancient times, cooks supposedly removed a single strand from the boiling water and threw it against the ceiling; if it stuck up there, it was done. (*Danger!* If there are no old spaghetti strands on the ceiling, *don't* try this method.) An alternate method is to simply taste the spaghetti; it should be chewy but not tough—*al dente.*

As the pasta completes its boil, grate the Parmesan cheese and put it into a small serving bowl. Mix the salad dressing, pour it over the greens, and toss the salad lightly. Take the spaghetti from the pot, drain it, place it on a serving platter, and drape the sauce artfully over it. Hold the Brie and crackers for a final course.

As the family digs in, pour the Chianti. This is one time your wife won't ask you what the celebration is. This time she'll know.

MENU 2

Chicken Teriyaki
Rice with Almonds
Sautéed Green Peppers
Sherbet

Don't ever give this recipe away. You'll be asked for it constantly, of course, but you must not weaken. Accept all compliments gracefully, but never, ever, give this recipe to anyone—because if you do, everyone will know just how little work you had to do.

Experienced cooks soon learn how to deflect these recipe requests. One of the traditional responses is to give away the reciple with one or two key ingredients missing. This tends to discourage future requests. A second and more charitable approach, one we have favored, requires a little white lie: "Recipe? What recipe? Oh, I just make it up as I go along. You know, a little bit of this and a little bit of that. . . ."

The Staples: Make sure that these are all on hand: fresh garlic, rice, dry sherry or dry white wine, butter.

The Shopping List: A three-pound broiling chicken (cut into very small pieces), Japanese soy sauce (large bottle), slivered almonds, one bunch scallions, four green peppers, a bunch of fresh parsley, one quart of sherbet. This should be enough for the average family of two adults and 2.2 children.

The key to this meal's success is the marinade, the sauce that the chicken soaks in before the cooking. Incidentally, the same sauce works as well with shrimp or sliced beef or lamb. Although the best time to make the marinade—and to start using it—is the night before the meal, you can begin the process just three hours before cooking the dinner.

The Night Before: Put a cup of soy sauce into a flat baking dish. Add some sherry or white wine—just a splash will do. Peel and mince three cloves of garlic and add them to the sauce. Chop a large handful of parsley as finely as possible and add that.

In time, you may want to experiment by adding other flavorings to the marinade. You might try a large pinch of freshly chopped ginger root, a spoonful of tomato sauce, a few dashes of Tabasco sauce, a little pineapple juice—but you can hold the experimentation for later efforts.

Place the chicken pieces in the marinade. (*Caution!* The chicken pieces must be small, what are commonly called "finger pieces.") Stir the marinade so that each piece of chicken is thoroughly coated with the sauce. (During the next twenty-four hours, you should stir the mixture a couple of times more, making sure that the chicken is recoated.) Cover the baking dish with plastic wrap and keep refrigerated until it is to be used. Then get a good night's sleep. Believe it or not, most of your work is done.

5:15 PM: Although Chicken Teriyaki is delicious when barbecued—using the marinade as a barbecue sauce—it is simpler to cook it in the oven. Pour the excess marinade off into a separate bowl and put the chicken under the broiler.

Broil for approximately fifteen minutes on each side. Then bake for half an hour in an oven set at 350 degrees. Every now and then, three or four times, baste the chicken with some of the marinade and turn over the pieces so that they are browned evenly on all sides. (*Danger!* Make sure that the chicken is not placed too close to the flame during the broiling process. One sure way to tell when it is too close: It will start to turn black.)

5:45 PM: Begin cooking the rice, following the directions on the package. (*Danger!* Make sure that you lower the temperature as soon as the water starts to boil.)

6 PM: Prepare the green peppers. Cut away the core and the seeds, then slice the green peppers into narrow strips. Peel the scallions and slice lengthwise, using the white and two inches of the green part of the scallions. Put the green peppers into a frying pan with a quarter stick of butter over medium heat and sauté. After five minutes or so, add the scallions. Stir occasionally.

6:20 PM: Check the rice. The water should be thoroughly absorbed. Add butter and a small handful of the slivered almonds.

6:30 PM: The green peppers are cooked; the rice is ready; the chicken browned, perhaps even slightly crispy. If it seems too soggy, put it under the broiler for a final turn. (*Danger!* This is no time to let your attention wander; the difference between crispy and up-in-smoke is about a minute.)

After that, it's just a matter of getting the dinner to the table in the proper sequence. And later, as you're serving the sherbet, someone will surely ask for the recipe. That's your big moment. "Recipe?" you say. "What recipe?"

MENU 3

Rock Cornish Game Hens in Grenadine
Apple Stuffing
Baked Carrots
Salad
Ice Cream

Sometimes it's not enough just to cook the dinner properly. There's also the matter of presenting it properly. What we're talking about now is public relations. This is especially true of tonight's meal.

When the kids go into the standard "What's-for-dinner?" routine, you're not likely to say something so unwieldy as "Rock Cornish game hens in grenadine." You may even be tempted to take the easy way out and say, "Chicken." Wrong! When in doubt, say "Squab." Now a Rock Cornish game hen is not exactly a squab. Nor is it precisely a chicken. The difference between a squab and a chicken, that's public relations.

The Staples: Make sure that these are all on hand: butter, sage, salt, pepper, and two lemons.

The Shopping List: Three Rock Cornish game hens, one quart apple juice, one small bottle grenadine syrup, two pounds fresh carrots, six celery stalks, two onions, one cucumber, three apples, parsley, one head lettuce, fresh dill, one small container sour cream, one large bag dry bread crumbs or stuffing mix, ice cream. This should be enough to feed a mob like yours.

Which comes first, the chicken or the stuffing? Well, since the stuffing is the major culinary challenge facing you tonight, we'll begin with that. And with this cautionary note: If you have purchased *frozen* Rock Cornish game hens, you must allow several hours for thawing them. Otherwise, there is not much you will be able to do with tonight's dinner, except maybe stick it in your highball.

5 PM: Melt half a stick of butter in a skillet over medium heat. Add two chopped onions and four chopped celery stalks and cook until tender. Place four or five cups of dry bread crumbs or stuffing mix in a large bowl and add the cooked onion and celery. Peel and core the three apples, cut them into small pieces, and add to the mixture. Also add a large pinch of sage, a small handful of chopped parsley, some salt and pepper, and the juice of one lemon. Now add enough apple juice to make the mixture moist and easily packed. A cup or two should do it. Pack the mix into the body cavities of the three game hens. Leftover stuffing can be wrapped in metal foil and baked beside the game hens.

5:15 PM: Preheat the oven to 350 degrees. Peel and slice the carrots.

5:30 PM: Place the three stuffed game hens in a shallow baking dish on a rack and paint them with grenadine syrup. Surround the game hens with mounds of sliced carrots dotted with butter and put the baking dish into the preheated oven.

Three or four times during the next hour, baste the birds

with fresh coatings of grenadine syrup. At the same time, stir the carrots into the juices of the game hens.

6 PM: Now, while you have a few moments, put together the salad. Make sure the lettuce is rinsed free of any sand and patted dry with paper towels before being broken into bite-sized pieces. Peel and slice a cucumber. Add a couple of stalks of celery, sliced.

Mix the sour cream with a small handful of freshly chopped dill. (If fresh dill is not available, try a large pinch of dill seed.) Add some salt, pepper, and a generous squeeze of lemon. You can, if you wish, substitute yogurt. (*Danger!* If using yogurt, make sure it is plain yogurt. There are few salad dressings less appetizing than one that is flavored with both dill and, oh, boysenberry yogurt.)

6:20 PM: Check the game hens, making sure that neither birds nor carrots are drying out. Add grenadine syrup, if necessary.

6:30 PM: Unless you have a jeweler's eyepiece, you will not attempt to carve a game hen the way you might carve a turkey. Nor will you entertain separate orders for white or dark meat. The easiest way to serve a game hen is to cut it in half, leaving the stuffing intact and arranging the carrots alongside. Incidentally, at this point it won't matter whether it's called chicken or squab. If you've done your part, it'll be called delicious.

MENU 4

Chili con Carne
Coleslaw
Iced Beer
Fruit in Season

If cooking can be called a science, it is an inexact science. Some people would have it otherwise—a quarter-of-a-teaspoon of this and an eighth-of-a-teaspoon of that—but these are the same kind of people who enjoy balancing checkbooks. Of all the dishes we're going to make together, this is one of the least exact.

A few years ago, a national magazine had the temerity to publish "the world's best chili recipe." Sheer nonsense. There is no *one* best chili recipe; there are dozens, hundreds. Fortunately, however, we will be serving this one in the company of the world's best coleslaw recipe.

The Staples: Make sure that these are all on hand: butter, vegetable oil, fresh garlic, chili powder, celery salt, cumin seeds, caraway seeds, oregano, cayenne pepper, salt, eggs, flour, sugar, mustard, and cider vinegar.

The Shopping List: One pound of dry kidney beans, two pounds of chuck steak (not counting the bone), four medium-sized onions, one large can of Italian plum tomatoes, one head of fresh cabbage, one small container of sour cream (or plain yogurt), beer, crackers, fruit in season.

The Night Before: Soak the beans overnight in cool water. There are some people who would tell you that you can get away with opening a can of precooked beans, but don't listen to them.

Early in the Day: Bring the beans to a low boil and then cut the heat back, allowing them to simmer until tender (about three to four hours). One way to test for tenderness is to blow on a bean and see if the skin breaks. (*Caution!* Since this looks at least mildly ridiculous, don't let anyone see you doing it.)

Also Early in the Day: As the beans are simmering, you can make the cooked dressing for the world's best coleslaw. This is a little tricky. If you bomb out, try it a second time. If you bomb out a second time, you may want to consider mayo with a splash of vinegar.

Melt a quarter stick of butter in a saucepan over low heat. (*Danger! Very* low heat, or else the eggs will scramble.) Add two beaten eggs, a large spoonful of sugar, a large dab of mustard, and half a cup of cider vinegar. Keep stirring gently over low heat. In ten minutes or so, it will thicken all at once and you will remove it from the heat. (*Danger!* If you don't remove it at once, you may want to feed it to the dog while it is still warm.) Add the sour cream (or yogurt) and put the dressing into the refrigerator to cool.

3:30 PM: Now, while the salad dressing is cooling, turn your attention to the chili itself. Chili sauce, like spaghetti sauce, lends itself to experimentation.

Begin by cutting the chuck steak into chunks and dusting

the chunks with flour. (The easiest way to do this is to put both meat and flour into a brown paper bag and shake.) Cook the meat in a small amount of oil over medium heat until it turns brown. Chop up the onions and mince the cloves of garlic, add this to the meat, and cook for five or ten minutes—just until the onions start to turn brown at the edges. Stir in half the tomatoes, then the spices—a pinch of celery salt, a large pinch of cumin seeds, another of oregano, a healthy dose of salt and cayenne pepper, and then the chili powder itself. Try two tablespoonfuls. Taste. Oh, add another one. (*Caution!* It is always easy to add chili powder, not so easy to subtract it.) Simmer the sauce over low heat until the meat is tender (at least two hours).

5:30 PM: Now add about half the precooked kidney beans. And taste. At this point you can add more beans, more tomatoes, or more chili powder—let your taste be your guide.

Grate or chop the cabbage. Add the dressing along with a small handful of caraway seeds. You have just made the world's best coleslaw.

There is nothing to do after this except serve the chili hot and the slaw cold, accompanied by enough beer to give your palate an occasional rinse. Why beer? Because wine with chili is about as appetizing as wine with pretzels.

MENU 5

Steak Diane
Baked Potatoes
Green Beans and Onions
Fresh Cherries

Whenever a fine chef makes Steak Diane, he turns it into a major production number. Most often he will cook it on a chafing dish right beside your table. There are the sizzling sounds of the steak, the pungent aromas of the special sauce, and then the chef produces a bottle of cognac, splashes the cognac into the frying pan, touches it with a match and . . . it's show time!

Okay, here's your chance to break into show business. But don't rush it. Just as the better Broadway show needs its out-of-town tryout, you'll want to run through this dinner a few times before trying it out for guests. Test your act on the less critical members of the immediate family. A mis-fired Steak Diane will leave the match sputtering unromantically in a damp bog of sauce and spice. Or, worse, you may go down in flames, creating the kind of explosion more suitable to the White Sands Proving Ground than to the dining room table.

The Staples: Make sure that these are all on hand: butter, salt, pepper, garlic, basil, Worcestershire sauce, Dijon mustard, sherry, cognac.

The Shopping List: Two pounds of steak, sliced thin and pounded flat (tell the butcher it's for Steak Diane), shallots (or chives, or scallions), parsley, two pounds of fresh green beans, lemon, an onion, two pounds of Idaho potatoes, fresh cherries.

We're keeping the side dishes as simple as possible tonight so that there will be nothing to distract you at the magic moment of ignition. It is possible to make Steak Diane without the flaming finale, of course, just as it's possible to celebrate the Fourth of July without fireworks.

5:15 PM: Preheat the oven to 350 degrees. While the oven is getting hot, carefully wash the potatoes. (*Caution! No* soap.) When the potatoes are clean and still wet, salt them heavily. Some like to coat the skins with melted butter before adding the salt, but that is just gilding the lily.

5:30 PM: Put the potatoes onto an open rack in the preheated oven. It should take about an hour to bake them. Rinse the green beans and cut off their tips. Put half a stick of butter into a large saucepan over medium heat. Add two cloves of garlic, minced. Sauté the garlic for five minutes with one medium chopped onion. Add the green beans, salt, pepper, and a pinch of basil. Cook over medium-low heat until the beans are tender, then turn the heat to low.

6 PM: There will come a time when you will be able to make the sauce for the Steak Diane at the same time as the steak. Not tonight. Tonight we'll make the sauce in advance and add it at the last minute. In a small saucepan over medium-low heat, melt half a stick of butter. Add a handful of chopped shallots (or chives, or scallions) and a few sprigs of parsley, chopped. Now a dash of salt and pepper, a couple of splashes of Worcestershire sauce, and a small spoonful of Dijon mustard. Keep this warm. Test the green beans for tenderness; squeeze half a lemon over them.

6:25 PM: This is it, the big moment. Break a leg, as they say in show biz. The steaks must be thin and free of fat. Heat a heavy frying pan over medium-high heat; add a dab of butter and a steak. Each steak should be cooked for a minute or two on each side over high heat. (*Caution!* Add more butter if the steaks start to stick.) Then place the steaks in a warm oven.

Put an ounce or so of cognac in a small saucepan over medium heat for a minute or so. Don't let it get too hot. Then pour it into the pan you used to fry the steaks. Match! Flames! Applause! Then, as the flames die out, add a healthy shot of sherry and scrape together the steak residues. Mix in the sauce you made earlier.

Test the baking potatoes with a fork. When the fork passes easily through the potatoes, they're ready.

Gently spoon the sauce over each steak and allow some to drip onto the potatoes. If all this has worked perfectly, there may be a curtain call or two. But if it hasn't, you simply follow the oldest culinary tradition of them all: The dinner must go on.

MENU 6

Beef Stroganoff
Noodles
Fresh Peas
Strawberries in Liqueur

Today I'm going to ask you to commit one of the culinary world's classic no-nos. Maybe *the* classic no-no. One thing that no self-respecting cook would ever do—or at least would ever *admit* to doing—is use ketchup as seasoning in a classy recipe. Hash houses use ketchup because it's the great pretender—it covers up mistakes and conceals mediocrity; in short, it hides the taste. Well, here it's going to add to the taste.

In using ketchup, there are two possible approaches. There is, of course, the brazen approach—you take the clearly labeled bottle from the pantry and calmly blast some of it into the pot. Then there's the discreet approach—early in the day, before the actual cooking commences, you pour a small amount of ketchup into a saucer and you thereafter refer to it as tomato sauce or, better still, as *sauce au tomate*.

The Staples: Make sure that these are all on hand: butter, garlic, flour, salt, pepper, white wine, a small amount of liqueur (preferably Cointreau or Grand Marnier), and finally—remember, not a word about this to anyone—some ketchup.

The Shopping List: Two and a half pounds of boneless steak (either filet mignon or round), three onions, one can beef bouillon, dill (fresh is best), one pint sour cream, one pound of flat noodles, one half pound fresh mushrooms, two pounds of peas (fresh, if possible), and one quart of strawberries (ditto).

First, take a deep breath. Relax. While I'll concede that Beef Stroganoff is somewhat more complicated than the dishes we've been cooking, it also happens to be nearly foolproof. Short of dropping the platter on the floor, there are few effective ways of ruining—or even seriously damaging—tonight's dinner for five.

5:20 PM: The key to cooking any complicated dish is getting some of the work out of the way before the fire is lit. Cut the beef into one-inch cubes. Chop the onions fine. Mince two cloves of garlic. Rinse the mushrooms, cut away the tips of the stems, and slice. Shell the fresh peas and place them in a separate bowl. Rinse the strawberries and cut away the stems.

5:40 PM: Heat a large frying pan over high heat. Add a quarter stick of butter and some of the meat chunks. Cook rapidly over high heat, stirring the meat so that it is browned on all sides. After a minute or two, transfer the meat to another dish. Add more butter and more meat to the frying pan and repeat.

Put six quarts of water into your largest kettle and place this over high heat; this will be for the noodles. In a small saucepan, heat two or three cups of water; this will be for the peas.

6 PM: Back to the Stroganoff. Add half a stick of butter to the frying pan and melt over medium heat. Put in the chopped onions and the minced garlic. Cook for a couple of minutes and then add the sliced mushrooms. Cook for an additional five minutes or so, stirring the mixture all the while.

At the beginning of this book, we promised to do away with exact measurements as much as possible. What you're going to do now is add some flour to the food in the pan. How much flour? Well, considerably more than a smidgen and somewhat less than a handful. Oh, the hell with it. Add three tablespoons of flour. Cook and stir a few seconds. Now take the frying pan away from the heat.

Now add a dash of the ketchup—or the *sauce au tomate,* whichever you prefer. Next add a few shakes of salt, a few grinds of pepper. Stir this together until the sauce has a reasonably smooth consistency.

When the water in the large pot is boiling, add the noodles slowly and follow the time directions printed on the package. When the water in the saucepan boils, add the shelled peas and cook over medium heat for approximately ten minutes before turning off the heat, draining, and adding butter.

6:15 PM: Put the frying pan back over medium heat and slowly add the can of undiluted beef bouillon. (*Caution!* Very slowly.) Do this while stirring the mixture. Bring it all to a slow boil and then reduce the heat to low at once and allow it to simmer.

6:25 PM: Time for the final checklist. The peas should be ready to serve. The noodles should be drained and placed on a serving platter.

Add to your sauce a healthy shot of white wine and the beef that was cooked earlier, and reheat. Then add a few teaspoons of minced dill. Shortly before serving, stir the container of sour cream into the sauce until it is well blended. (*Danger!* Do not allow the sauce to boil after this point. There are very few ways of ruining the dinner and that is one of them.)

6:30 PM: Serve the Stroganoff over the noodles and scatter some fresh dill over the top. For dessert, you'll have strawberries served with a touch of brandy. And now you can put the ketchup back where it belongs, right next to the sign that says "For Emergency Use Only."

MENU 7

Roast Beef with Horseradish Sauce
Yorkshire Pudding
Tomato-and-Onion Salad
Cheshire Cheese and Apple Slices

There are some who would call this a classic English dinner. Unfortunately, most seasoned travelers would rank the classic English dinner right up there with the Gobi Desert on the list of all-time overrated tourist attractions.

The truth is this: A visitor wandering through the inns and hostels of England could order this meal a dozen nights in a row and never come close to the Yorkshire Pudding you're going to make tonight, your first time out.

In Yorkshire, where they should surely know better, the pudding is often a glutinous yellow substance that settles into your stomach like freshly poured concrete. Incidentally, in Yorkshire it is served as a separate course just before the roast beef. This causes many visitors to lose their appetite by the time the meat arrives—and sometimes that's just as well. All too often the roast beef has been cooked to a uniform grayness and dried thoroughly before being sent to your table.

The Staples. Make sure that these are all on hand: salt, pepper, milk, flour, eggs, butter, wine vinegar, mustard, salad oil.

The Shopping List: A six- to eight-pound rib roast, one can of beef bouillon, one small bottle of white horseradish, three large ripe tomatoes, two Bermuda onions, three apples, half a pound of Cheshire (or cheddar) cheese.

4:30 PM: Preheat the oven to 350 degrees. Rub salt and pepper into the surface of the roast beef and stand it upright in a baking pan. If you like your meat rare, allow about eighteen minutes a pound—roughly an hour and three quarters for a six-pound roast. For medium, add another four minutes per pound.

4:45 PM: Place the roast in the oven.

Tonight's salad is an easy one, thin slices of tomato alternating with thin slices of onion. After arranging the slices on a serving platter, mix up a simple vinaigrette salad dressing and set it aside until later: Use three or four parts of salad oil to one part of wine vinegar and then add some salt, pepper, a teaspoon of mustard, and, if you're in the mood, a pinch of minced garlic or basil.

5:20 PM: And now the horseradish sauce. In a saucepan heat the can of undiluted beef bouillon over medium-high heat. In a separate saucepan, melt three tablespoons of butter over medium-low heat. Add the same amount of flour and stir together until smooth. As soon as the bouillon reaches the boiling point, add it to the butter-flour mixture and stir. It will thicken immediately. Remove the saucepan from the heat and add three tablespoons of horseradish. Add more if your taste tells you it needs it. Keep the sauce warm over very low heat and stir occasionally.

5:30 PM: Sharpen your carving knife.

5:45 PM: You are now ready to construct tonight's *pièce de résistance,* the Yorkshire Pudding. Although you can do this with a hand mixer, the easiest way is to use a blender.

Break two eggs into the blender and beat them for twenty or thirty seconds. Now add a cup of milk to the beaten eggs and blend the milk and eggs together. To this foamy mix, add a couple of dashes of salt, a couple of tablespoons of roast beef drippings, and a cup of flour. Blend all this together just until the mixture is smooth.

Either a cake pan or a soufflé dish will work for the Yorkshire Pudding. Add a couple of spoons of beef drippings and allow them to coat the surface of the baking dish. Pour in the batter to a depth of about half an inch.

6:10 PM: Put the batter into a very hot oven—turn the heat up to 450 degrees for the first ten minutes and then down to 350 degrees for the final fifteen minutes. If it's necessary to remove the roast beef while the Yorkshire Pudding is cooking, that's all right. The beef will continue to cook in its own juices until the pudding is ready.

6:30 PM: Carve the roast beef and serve with the horseradish sauce on the side. Pour the well-mixed salad dressing over the tomatoes and onions.

And now open the oven. There you should find the perfect Yorkshire Pudding, slightly moist at the center but light and high at the edges, the kind of culinary triumph that would cause any resident of Yorkshire to say, "Hey, what is this stuff?" For dessert: slices of apple and Cheshire (or cheddar) cheese.

MENU 8

Tuna Rockefeller
Rice with Parsley
Grilled Tomatoes
Chocolate Stuff

I've heard complaints from some wives. They're pleased when their husbands actually cook a meal. However, they're not so pleased by what happens *after* dinner. After dinner the kitchen looks like a battlefield in a Civil War movie, like a junkyard in the wake of a tornado—mountains of pots and pans waiting there for the Dishwashing Genie to make her nightly appearance.

Come on, guys, this can't go on. Fair's fair, after all. If in the past one member of the family has been silly enough to both cook the dinner and wash the dishes, you have no choice in this matter. On those nights that you cook dinner, you have to face up to your full responsibility and bribe one of the kids to do the dishes.

And since you may need extra cash for that bribe, tonight's meal is a penny pincher's special. Tuna Rockefeller is a low-budget rip-off of Oysters Rockefeller—if you love Oysters Rockefeller you're going to like Tuna Rockefeller. Similarly, if you love chocolate mousse, you're sure to like tonight's Chocolate Stuff. The difference between the two is measured in man-hours—*your* man-hours.

The Staples: Make sure that these are all on hand: sugar, vanilla, egg, salt, pepper, milk, lemon, butter.

The Shopping List: Two seven-ounce cans of white-meat tuna, half a pound of bacon, flavored bread crumbs, one pound fresh spinach, one bunch parsley, one box brown rice, four large ripe tomatoes, four ounces grated Parmesan cheese, one small container sour cream, eight ounces semi-sweet chocolate, brandy (optional), instant coffee (optional).

4:30 PM: Since the dessert requires some time in the refrigerator, we'll begin with that.

Put one cup of milk into a saucepan over medium heat. Into the blender goes the semisweet chocolate, broken up into small chunks. Add a teaspoon of vanilla and, if you like, a couple of teaspoons of sugar. Break an egg into the blender. If you should happen to have a bottle of brandy nearby, a shot of brandy will only improve matters. And if you like the flavor of coffee mixed with chocolate, you might consider adding a teaspoon of instant coffee.

Oops, the *milk!* As the milk reaches the boiling point, remove it from the heat. (*Danger!* If you happen to be looking the other way, you will turn around to see a Niagara of boiling milk cascading over your stove.) Pour the scalded milk directly into the blender.

After a minute or so, turn on the blender until the chocolate mixture is smooth. Pour into dessert dishes and place in the refrigerator.

5:15 PM: Rinse the spinach carefully in a pot of clear water. Do it a second time. Cook the spinach in a covered saucepan containing a small amount of water boiling over medium-high heat. In just a few moments, when the spinach is soft, drain it and chop it as fine as you can. You may want to run it through the blender—but only *after* the chocolate has been washed away.

Fry the bacon in a large frying pan over medium heat, turning the bacon once and then draining it on paper towels. Put the chopped spinach into a baking dish and add the bacon, crumbled into pieces. Then add half a cup of the seasoned bread crumbs, about half the grated Parmesan cheese, half the sour cream, some salt and pepper, and the juice of half a lemon. Finally, open the cans of tuna fish, drain away the liquid, and flake the tuna into the mixture. Stir this up. Sprinkle the rest of the Parmesan cheese over the top.

Preheat the oven to 350 degrees.

5.45 PM: Tonight may well mark your family's introduction to brown rice as opposed to white rice. The main difference between the two is that brown rice has not been polished and refined and stripped of its vitamins. However, since it is a scientific fact that all kids instinctively choose unhealthy food over healthy food, you may be subjecting yourself to some personal criticism here.

It's up to you to guide your family past the health-food barrier. Follow the cooking directions on the rice box and then, just before serving, add a fistful of minced parsley, a large slab of butter, and some salt and pepper. If that doesn't work, try some chives, or some cooked onions, or some Parmesan cheese, or almost anything else you can lay your hands on.

6 PM: Rinse the tomatoes, cut them in halves, and sprinkle them with salt, pepper, dots of butter, and some of the bread crumbs.

6:10 PM: Put the Tuna Rockefeller into the oven; it will be ready in twenty minutes.

6:20 PM: Grill the tomato halves under the broiler for a few minutes, just until the bread crumbs have turned brown.

6:30 PM: Final steps. Check the Chocolate Stuff in the refrigerator; it should be firm and well chilled. The tomatoes and the rice are hot and the Tuna Rockefeller is ready. Anything else? Just one little thing. Take the pots and pans and place them in a basin of hot, soapy water. This is for use *after* the dinner is eaten.

MENU 9

Guacamole
Tacos
Beer
Melon

Okay, it's your turn to cook dinner but . . . nothing seems right. They happen to the best of cooks, those evenings when you draw a blank and time is running out. What to do? Well, why not just start cooking now and ask questions later?

Fine, but cook *what*? You might consider the basic, all-purpose starter meal. Slice some onions into a frying pan. Add a chopped pepper, some minced garlic, some salt and pepper, some chopped tomatoes, some ground meat. At this point, your background takes over. If you happen to be Italian, you'll reach for the oregano and the spaghetti. Indian— and you'll want some curry and rice. Hungarians will go for noodles and paprika.

But on this particular night, the accent is Mexican. Tonight you'll rely on the south-of-the-border spices and make tacos that will be the envy of fast-food stands everywhere.

The Staples: Make sure that these are all on hand: garlic, oregano, chili powder, cumin, coriander, Tabasco sauce, salt, pepper, butter.

The Shopping List: One pound ground beef, one large on-ion, three tomatoes, one package tortillas (frozen or dried), two green chili peppers (carefully seeded), one half pound cheddar cheese, one head iceberg lettuce, one small can to-mato sauce, two ripe avocados, one melon, one lemon, one lime, beer.

Any taco recipe quickly becomes the original creation of the person doing the cooking. It's one of those meals that you bend to your own taste almost immediately. So what follows should not be considered a recipe so much as a start-ing point.

5:30 PM: The way you start the taco sauce is much the way you start a spaghetti sauce. Begin by frying the ground beef in a large frying pan over medium heat. When the meat is browned, drain away the fat and set the beef to one side. Let me remind you again: Do not drain the fat into the sink. *Never* drain fat into a sink.

Melt a chunk of butter in the frying pan and add half the onion, chopped fine; two tomatoes, chopped; two cloves of garlic, minced; and the seeded green chili peppers, minced. Simmer this over medium heat for ten minutes and then add the tomato sauce. Add a pinch of oregano, a pinch of cumin, and another of coriander.

And now the chili powder. How much chili powder? Well, before making a decision of this magnitude, you must ask yourself this question: How much cold beer do you have on hand?

Try two tablespoons of chili powder, more if you like things hot. Finally, add the cooked meat. Keep the mixture warm over very low heat until you serve it.

5:50 PM: Grate the cheddar cheese and chop half a head of lettuce. Set both aside.

Cook the tortillas, following the directions on the package. Whether you choose the dried or frozen form, you'll wind up with a corn pancake that forms a pocket for the taco filling.

6 PM: Guacamole is traditionally served as an appetizer, a dip that is generally accompanied by crackers. Tonight, however, it will be your salad. Make the guacamole as close to dinnertime as possible, as it has an unfortunate tendency to turn brownish.

Rub the inside of a small bowl with a peeled clove of garlic and then throw it away. (The garlic, not the bowl.) Peel the ripe avocados and mash them with a fork. Add the juice of half a lemon, the rest of the chopped onion, a few dashes of Tabasco sauce, freshly ground pepper, salt, and one medium-sized tomato, chopped fine.

6:30 PM: When a meal is this simple to put together, appearance counts. Serve the chilled beer in proper glasses. Scoop the guacamole onto a nice bed of lettuce. Serve the melon slices with a wedge of lime.

The tacos themselves will have to be individual creations. The meat mixture is spooned inside the folded tortilla and is then topped by a handful of chopped lettuce and grated cheese.

Now bite into it. Ah! It should be spicy—hot to the mouth and warm to the stomach. And it should be followed, in short order, by a long beer. For this is a scientific fact: The only known antidote to the well-made taco is the properly chilled beer.

MENU 10

Tarragon Chicken
New Potatoes
Greens with Perfect French Dressing
Vanilla Ice Cream with Crème de Menthe

A woman known to be a first-rate cook had one idiosyncrasy—she always removed the legs from the chicken before cooking it. Finally, one of her dinner guests asked what happened to the drumsticks. The woman explained that this was the proper way to cook a chicken, the *only* way to cook a chicken. It was, in fact, the way her dear mother had always cooked chickens, and her mother was the best cook in the entire county. The guest was still curious about this, and she telephoned the woman's mother and asked her what culinary benefits came your way when you cooked legless chickens. The old woman thought for a moment and said, "Oh, yes, the reason I cut the legs off was that I didn't have a pot big enough for the whole chicken."

In such a way are culinary traditions established. And that's the danger of slavishly following patterns: Whole generations miss out on drumsticks.

The truth is that there is more than one way to roast a bird. Tonight's seasoning, for example, is tarragon, but it could as easily be rosemary or marjoram, thyme or paprika.

Different tastes, but the same overall result.

The Staples: Make sure that these are all on hand: salt, pepper, Dijon mustard, garlic, wine vinegar, olive oil, vegetable oil, eggs, tarragon (either fresh or dried), crème de menthe.

The Shopping List: Three pounds of new potatoes, two four-pound roasting chickens, half a pound of bacon, one head of lettuce, one bunch watercress, two large lemons, one small container sour cream, vanilla ice cream. (If new potatoes aren't available, any potatoes will do.)

4:30 PM: Preheat the oven to 450 degrees. Rub the juice of one lemon over the two chickens, both inside and out. Inside the roasting chickens you are apt to find a small packet of spare parts (neck, gizzard, liver, and so forth). Take this out and set it aside for another day, in the refrigerator, please. But leave the legs on.

Now take a healthy pinch of tarragon and scatter it within the body cavity of each chicken. Sprinkle another pinch over the outside of the birds. Then add a scattering of salt and pepper. Place the two chickens on a metal rack in a shallow baking pan; the metal rack keeps the birds from getting soggy. Lay the strips of bacon over the chickens, put them into the preheated oven, and lower the temperature to 350 degrees.

5 PM: Boil the unpeeled potatoes in a pot of water for about ten minutes. Remove them from the heat and allow them to cool off before going back to them. Spoon some of the drippings over the roasting chickens. The bacon will be cooked on one side; turn over the strips but leave them on the birds and return the roasting pan to the oven.

5:15 PM: Rinse the greens—the lettuce, the watercress, and any other salad ingredients you care to add—and pat them dry with paper towels.

Now you're ready to make the Perfect French Dressing. You can use either a blender or a jar with a tight cap.

Start with a large pinch of salt and a healthy dose of black pepper, freshly ground if possible. Add two teaspoons of Dijon mustard, the juice of a large lemon, four cloves of finely chopped garlic, a quarter cup of good wine vinegar, a quarter cup of olive oil, a cup of vegetable oil, two eggs that have been beaten, and, finally, the sour cream. Mix. This will be enough for a few salads, and it will keep nicely in the refrigerator.

5:30 PM: Back to the chickens. Remove the bacon slices and drain them on paper towels. Break the cooked bacon into small pieces and add them to the salad greens. Put the chickens back into the oven without the bacon, and baste them every fifteen minutes or so with drippings from the bottom of the pan.

5:45 PM: The new potatoes should be sufficiently cool now so that the skins will peel away easily. Place the peeled potatoes in the oven with the chickens, allowing the spuds to complete their cooking in the same juices that you use for basting. When you baste the birds, turn the potatoes over so that they brown evenly on all sides.

6:20 PM: Test the chickens for doneness. The easiest way to do this is to wiggle one of the legs—if it moves easily in its hip socket, it is ready. A fork should easily pierce the potatoes. And now is the proper time to add the dressing to the salad, tossing the greens to make sure they're all coated. The ice cream will be served later with a dash of crème de menthe.

And now, as you prepare to carve the chickens, you can take requests for drumsticks. There should be precisely four of them. Any more or any less and you haven't been paying attention.

MENU 11

Caesar Salad
Fettucini Alfredo
Iced Coffee
After-Dinner Mints

We tend to make too much of our cooking. Often we exaggerate the importance of the small detail, the not entirely essential nicety. Tonight's meal is a case in point.

Most recipes for Caesar Salad seem designed to scare off the amateurs. One cookbook insists that the salad be served on "properly chilled" plates. Another tells us to be particularly careful when tossing the salad lest we "bruise" the lettuce. Well, I have strong doubts about this sort of thing. I'm not sure what the proper chill factor for a plate is. Moreover, I've given Caesar Salads some fairly violent tossings, possibly causing both bruises and internal injuries, but I've yet to hear a complaint.

Fettucini Alfredo is the famous dish that once caused Douglas Fairbanks and Mary Pickford to extend a vacation in Rome. When Alfredo was invited to introduce the dish to the New World, he left nothing to chance. Alfredo arrived in the city of Cincinnati carrying his own special flour for the noodles. He brought along aged Parmesan cheese from Italy. He insisted on imported peppercorns. He personally tested the butter, the cream, the eggs. And finally, when all was just so, he rolled out the noodles, cooked them in fiercely boiling water, stirred in the sauce, and passed his creation to the culinary experts who were on hand. They could only gasp out their admiration. At last, the perfect pasta! Alfredo, however, was making a face.

"It was the water," he muttered. "I should have brought the water from Rome." Now that strikes me as carrying things too far.

The Staples: Make sure that these are all on hand: wine vinegar, garlic, salt, pepper, one egg, one large lemon, Worcestershire sauce, Tabasco sauce, Dijon mustard, butter, coffee.

The Shopping List: One loaf of day-old Italian bread, two heads of romaine lettuce, one two-ounce can of anchovies, one half cup of olive oil, one half pound of grated Parmesan cheese, one pound of fettucini noodles, one half cup of fresh cream, after-dinner mints.

Prepare in Advance: The croutons for the salad. Your supermarket doubtless carries several brands of packaged croutons. Try not to think about this fact.

Start with the loaf of Italian bread. Slice away the crusts and cut the bread into bite-sized cubes. Melt half a stick of butter in a large frying pan over medium heat and add two cloves of minced garlic. Sauté the bread cubes in the garlic butter, stirring them until they are browned all over. Set aside until ready to use.

5:30 PM: Tonight's first course will be the Caesar Salad, and it should be completely prepared—but not assembled—before you turn your attention to the fettucini.

Take the romaine lettuce, rinse clean, pat dry with paper

towels, and keep refrigerated until ready to serve.

Make the salad dressing in a jar with a tight cap. Begin with two cloves of minced garlic. Purists will advise taking the garlic and mashing it into the sides of a salad bowl with the heel of a spoon; it's precisely this kind of extra effort we're going to be avoiding tonight.

Add the juice of a large lemon, a tablespoon of wine vinegar, and the olive oil. Then add a couple of dashes of Worcestershire sauce, a few drops of Tabasco sauce, a teaspoon of Dijon mustard, and the egg, which has been cooked in boiling water for just one minute. The dressing is set aside until the last moment, then poured into the salad with the other ingredients.

Incidentally, you should know that the classic way of preparing a Caesar Salad is to start with a bowl of lettuce and simply add one ingredient after another. This makes for a good show until you break the nearly raw egg over the salad, at which time several of your kids will lose their appetites.

6 PM: Start a pot of coffee going. For a change of pace this is going to be served on ice, after dinner, with the mints.

6:10 PM: Start the water boiling in your largest pot. This will be for the noodles. Follow the cooking directions on the package of fettucini, using the minimum recommended time.

6:30 PM: As the water comes to a boil, throw in the fettucini, and then serve the first course, the salad. Break the lettuce into bite-sized pieces and place in a salad bowl. Add the anchovies, cut into small pieces, and then the croutons. Pour the dressing over the salad and add half the Parmesan cheese. Toss it gently, so as to leave the lettuce unmaimed.

(*Caution!* A word of warning on the anchovies: Go light with them if the kids have never seen anchovies before.)

As the salad is being eaten, the fettucini is boiling. You may have to interrupt your first course to go out for the final steps. Drain the noodles and place them in a large bowl with half a stick of butter and half a cup of cream and the rest of the Parmesan cheese. Add salt and a generous amount of freshly ground black pepper. Stir all this together. I'm not sure whether you have to worry about bruising the noodles or not. No, put that fear right out of your mind. In just about a minute, they're going to be irrevocably damaged.

MENU 12

Ernest Hemingway's Gazpacho
Meat Loaf
Herbed Bread
Watermelon

I'm beginning to wonder when Ernest Hemingway found time to write all those books. So far I've come up with five separate recipes called "Ernest Hemingway's Gazpacho" and, interestingly enough, the five recipes barely resemble one another.

But maybe that's the way it should be. Gazpacho, a chilled half-soup, half-salad, changes dramatically from one Spanish-speaking region to another. Sometimes it's almost a clear broth; other times it's thicker. However, here, in the best of the many Ernest Hemingway recipes, the vegetables are chopped fine to become part of the world's crunchiest soup.

Gazpacho is the perfect way to start a summertime meal—not only does it feed a mob, but it cools off a mob. It's a beautiful way to set up the hot herbed bread and the cold meat loaf that follow.

The Staples: Make sure that these are all on hand: olive oil, vinegar, white bread (four slices), butter, salt, pepper, thyme, garlic, eggs, cognac.

The Shopping List: One bunch of celery, six medium tomatoes, two bunches of scallions, two large green peppers, one medium cucumber, two medium onions, one bunch parsley, half a watermelon, two loaves Italian bread, one large can plum tomatoes, one large can tomato juice, one pound ground beef, one pound ground veal and pork (mixed), bread crumbs, one half pound bacon.

Tonight's supper, with the exception of the herbed bread, should be made the day before.

The Day Before: Use your largest bowl. Mince three cloves of garlic and mash them against the bowl with the heel of your spoon. Cut the crusts from the white bread and add the slices to the bowl. Pour half a cup of vinegar over the bread and mash all of this together until it forms a paste.

Stir in about half the canned tomatoes. Now chop fine the rest of the vegetables—the fresh tomatoes, the celery (without the leaves), the peeled cucumber, a bunch of scallions (with some of the green), one onion, and one seeded green pepper. Add these to the bowl with a quart of tomato juice and two cups of water. Refrigerate.

Also the Day Before: The meat loaf. Preheat the oven to 350 degrees. Sauté one chopped onion and one chopped green pepper in a little olive oil over medium heat until they are tender. Put the ground meat into a large bowl. Add two beaten eggs, the sautéed pepper and onion, a shot of cognac, and a large handful of bread crumbs. Chop up the parsley and add half of it, along with a liberal dose of salt and pepper and a healthy pinch of thyme. And, finally, more bread crumbs if the mixture seems too runny. Blend this together with your hands.

Place half the bacon strips across the bottom of a large

bread pan and pack the mixture into the pan. Place the other bacon strips over the meat loaf and bake it for ninety minutes at 350 degrees. Later, as the cooked meat loaf is cooling, cover it with foil, then put a second bread pan over the first and weight it down to compress the meat loaf. Refrigerate until ready to use.

6 PM: Now all you have to do on the night of the dinner is prepare the herbed bread. Preheat the oven to 350 degrees. Melt a stick of butter over medium heat and add two cloves of minced garlic, the rest of the minced parsley, and a handful of chopped scallions. Slice the Italian bread lengthwise, butter it with the mixture, and heat it in the oven for ten minutes or so, just until the bread starts to turn brown at the edges. The bread will be served with the meat loaf, sliced thin. And it will be followed by the watermelon.

And of course it will be preceded by bowls of Ernest Hemingway's Gazpacho, decorated with ice cubes and/or croutons. This should dispel all notions that cooking is not one of your more manly arts. Hemingway, of course, chased bulls and fought wars and tracked down big game and still found time to make gazpacho. That's right, guys, *macho gazpacho!*

MENU 13

Chicken Breasts Florentine
Rice in Bouillon
Rhubarb Pie
Turkish Coffee

There is a famous old cartoon: your basic middle-class family seated around the dinner table, the boy snarling at his parents, "I say it's spinach and I say to hell with it!"

We can't be sure what was said to set off this outburst. But I can imagine the well-bred mother saying, "Eat your *épinards*, dear." Or maybe the boy asked what he was eating and the father said, "That? Oh, that's chicken Florentine." Or eggs Florentine. Or almost-anything-at-all Florentine.

Whenever someone slips the word "Florentine" into a cooking conversation, it's just a slightly pompous way of saying "with spinach." It would have been as accurate to call this "chicken with spinach"—but a dish this good deserves just a touch of pomposity.

Incidentally, if the kid in the cartoon grew up to enjoy cooking, you can be sure he changed his attitude. It doesn't take long for a cook to develop Popeye's respect for spinach—not just for the way it can stand on its own but for its social nature, the way it mixes into almost any surrounding.

The Staples: Make sure that these are all on hand: salt, pepper, marjoram, butter, lemon, sherry, rice, flour, sugar.

The Shopping List: Two pounds of boneless chicken breasts, one pound fresh spinach, one bunch fresh rhubarb, one bunch scallions, one can chicken bouillon, one frozen piecrust, one small can Turkish or Greek coffee.

5 PM: The last shall come first. Although the rhubarb pie can be made earlier in the day, there's no need to go to that trouble.

Preheat the oven to 450 degrees. Rinse off the rhubarb stalks and chop them into small chunks. You'll need about four cups of the fruit. Mix the rhubarb pieces with one and a half cups of sugar, the juice of half a lemon, and a small fistful of white flour.

For years we've heard women discuss the difficulty of achieving the perfect piecrust. The sad truth is that this concern is well founded. And that is why today we're going to use a frozen piecrust, following the directions on the package.

5:15 PM: Spoon your fruit mixture into the pie shell and cover with a top crust. Put the pie into the oven.

5:25 PM: Lower the oven temperature to 350 degrees. The pie should be baked in forty minutes.

5:30 PM: The most difficult part of the meal will be the chicken, so we'll turn to that next. Rinse the chicken breasts under cool water and pat them dry with paper towels.

Put a cup of flour into a mixing bowl, add a dash of salt and pepper, then dust each chicken breast in the flour. Melt half a stick of butter in a large frying pan over medium heat and then add the chicken breasts. Sprinkle marjoram generously over each breast and cook for six or seven minutes on each side. (*Danger!* An overcooked chicken breast is a tough chicken breast.)

Add a splash of sherry and swirl it around the frying pan. When most of the wine has cooked away, put the chicken breasts into an ovenproof dish.

6 PM: Make rice according to the box directions, substituting the can of chicken bouillon for an equal amount of water and adding a handful of chopped scallions at the same time as you put in the rice.

6:05 PM: Remove the pie from the oven and replace it with the chicken. Turn the oven down to 250 degrees. Okay, the chicken is hot in the oven and the rice is cooking over very low heat. What now? Now the spinach. One thing you should know about fresh spinach; it's sandy. Even when the package says it has been rinsed, it is sometimes sandy. Rinse each leaf in a container of cool water—and once again.

Chop the spinach and put it into the frying pan you used for the chicken breasts. Over medium heat cook the spinach in the wine and butter and chicken scrapings left there from your earlier efforts. If the frying pan seems to be drying out, feel free to add another chunk of butter, another splash of wine, or both. In fact, do this even if the pan isn't drying out. The spinach will cook in about five minutes.

6:20 PM: Mix the spinach and the pan residues in with the chicken and keep it hot in the oven. It is difficult to tell whether the juices from the chicken lend flavor to the spinach or whether it's the other way around—either way, it's one of those rare marriages that improve both participants.

6:30 PM: Check the rice. Add butter. Remove the chicken from the oven and squeeze a lemon half over the dish.

After dinner, just before serving the rhubarb pie, sneak back into the kitchen and make some Turkish coffee. Although it is simple to make, it is rare enough to offer a perfect finishing touch to the meal.

To two cups of water add eight teaspoons of the finely pulverized coffee and an equal amount of sugar. Let the coffee come to a boil and pour the froth that forms into demitasse cups. Then put the coffee back on for another quick boil. Fill the small cups with the second supply of froth and serve. (*Danger!* Do not stir the coffee once it has been poured because what you will have then will not be coffee; its name will be mud.)

MENU 14

Ratatouille
Spaghetti alla Carbonara
Broiled Peach Halves

Many years ago Al Capp, the cartoonist who invented Li'l Abner, also invented something called a Shmoo. The Shmoo was mankind's ultimate pet. A small, eternally cheerful beast, the Shmoo gave service with a smile; he provided both milk and meat; you kicked a Shmoo and he was grateful for the attention. Not the least of their qualities was fecundity; they proliferated like rabbits gone berserk. And finally, like most do-gooders, they managed to make a bloody nuisance of themselves.

One can't be sure where Al Capp got his inspiration for the Shmoo. However, did you ever notice how much they resembled zucchinis?

Summer is the time of the zucchini, the elongated dark green squash that appears mysteriously in gardens everywhere. Not only does it appear; it grows—mushrooming overnight from blossom to grotesquerie. Leave your garden for a day and you will find that zucchinis have taken over whole sections, leaning against your string beans, sprawling over your strawberries, crushing your corn. Pick one zucchini and two new ones will appear.

Of course, you cook as many as you can. And then you

start giving them away to friends, to neighbors, to strangers, to anyone. There is one sensible solution to the zucchini explosion. It is called ratatouille—pronounced "rat-a-*too*-ee"— and it is a vegetable stew that is good either hot or cold; it can easily be a meal by itself on a warm summer's night.

The Staples: Make sure that these are all on hand: olive oil, garlic, salt, pepper, eggs, butter, dry white wine, brown sugar.

The Shopping List: Three medium onions, one small eggplant, four zucchinis, three green peppers, five large ripe tomatoes, one half pound bacon, one bunch parsley, one quarter pound Parmesan cheese, one pound spaghetti, six large ripe peaches.

5 PM: Take two of the onions, peel them, and chop them into small pieces. (If your eyes start to tear, try peeling the onions under cool running water.)

Now the green peppers. Cut away the seeds and slice the peppers into narrow strips. (If your eyes start to tear at this point, you're just unhappy.) Put a splash of olive oil into a large pan over medium heat and add the chopped onions and the peppers. Now add two cloves of garlic, minced fine. Cook for six or seven minutes, until the onions seem tender.

Slice the zucchinis crosswise, making the slices about a quarter of an inch in thickness. Peel the eggplant, cut it into bite-sized cubes, and add both the zucchinis and the eggplant to the pan.

While these vegetables are all stewing together, peel the tomatoes. No, not that way. The easiest way to peel a tomato is to dip it briefly into boiling water and then rinse it under cold water. The skin will slide away easily. Some purists would suggest that you remove the tomato seeds, but I've never been able to figure out how that's done. Cut the tomatoes into small chunks and add them to the pan along with some salt, pepper, and a small fistful of minced parsley.

The ratatouille can be keep simmering over very low heat until dinnertime. Or it can be stored in the refrigerator and served cold.

5:45 PM: Start the spaghetti water boiling in your largest pot—four to six quarts of water for a pound of spaghetti.

Peel an onion and chop it fine, then sauté it in a little oil in a saucepan over medium heat. In four or five minutes add the bacon, cut into small pieces. Cook for five or six minutes more, then add half a cup of dry white wine.

In a second bowl, beat two eggs and then add the grated Parmesan cheese, salt, and a generous amount of freshly ground pepper.

6:20 PM: Add the spaghetti to the briskly boiling water and cook it for the minimum recommended time on the box, until it is cooked through but chewy.

6:30 PM: Make sure that the ratatouille is hot (if it's supposed to be hot) or cold (if that's your plan).

As the spaghetti finishes cooking, drain it and transfer it to a large bowl. Immediately add the egg-and-cheese mixture and toss it together. Next add the bacon-and-onion mixture and toss it all together one more time.

The only trick to a meal like this is one of timing, of getting the various dishes cooked and served on some kind of schedule. Should either the spaghetti or the ratatouille not be completed on schedule, there's one easy solution—simply serve the dinner as two separate courses.

Five or ten minutes before the end of the meal, steal out

to the kitchen and peel the peaches the same way that you peeled the tomatoes. Cut them into halves. Take out the pits. Spoon brown sugar over each half and add a dab of butter. Put them under the broiler for just a few minutes, just until the butter is melted and the peaches are heated through. You can serve the peaches with cream, with whipped cream, with brandy, with flaming brandy, or just by themselves, leaving well enough alone.

MENU 15

Barbecued Shish Kebab
Wilted Spinach Salad
Iced Tea
Nectarines

Three quarters of a century ago, Richard Blechynden, an Englishman, decided to show Americans the proper way to brew a cup of tea. He set up his tea booth at the St. Louis World's Fair and waited for the customers. Unfortunately, the St. Louis temperature got up near 100 degrees and stayed there. Blechynden's tea was brisk, but his business was not.

One day while killing time, which Blechynden was doing a lot of that summer, he took to pitching chunks of ice into his kettle of perfectly brewed tea. Absentmindedly, he took a sip. Then a second. Hmmm. Maybe just a little more lemon and sugar. The rest, as they say, is history. In no time at all Richard Blechynden and his newly invented iced tea became the sensations of the St. Louis World's Fair.

The odd thing about the iced tea you're going to make tonight, it's even easier. Stay tuned.

The Staples: Make sure that these are all on hand: garlic, sugar, olive oil, white wine vinegar, salt, pepper, thyme, red wine, Worcestershire sauce, Dijon mustard. Also half a dozen skewers for barbecuing.

The Shopping List: Two pounds fresh spinach, one half pound bacon, a leg of lamb, boned (approximately seven pounds before boning), seven large onions, three lemons, six green peppers, one pound large mushrooms, one pound cherry tomatoes, one small tin of tea leaves (not tea bags), nectarines.

Prepare the Day Before: The marinade for the lamb. Mix one cup of red wine with half a cup of olive oil and one fourth cup of lemon juice. Add one onion, chopped fine, three minced garlic cloves, a large pinch of thyme, and a generous amount of salt and pepper.

Cut the lamb into two-inch cubes and soak the cubes in the marinade overnight. Several times during the course of the next twenty-four hours, turn the meat pieces over.

Also to Be Prepared the Day Before: The iced tea. The very notion of *instant* iced tea is a comment on our times. What could be more instant than plain, old-fashioned, regular tea—just add boiling water, right? Still, this isn't enough for an Instant Culture so all-encompassing as our own. We had to find a way to make instant tea even more instant— never mind that it requires the addition of "flavor enhancers," preservatives, additives, and other ingredients better suited to a laboratory.

One perfectly acceptable way to make iced tea, of course, is to brew a cup of regular hot tea and add ice—the original Richard Blechynden formula. However, since this is clearly too much work for most of us, here's a simpler method. The only catch: It must be made a day before you drink it.

Begin with a quart of cold water. Add five heaping teaspoons of tea leaves. Put this into the refrigerator and wait. That's all there is to it. No cooking. No muss, no fuss, no bother.

And now, on to the feast.

5 PM: Begin the barbecue fire.

Cut the green peppers into square pieces and five of the onions into wedges. Cut the caps away from the mushroom stems. Thread the food on the skewers—alternating the meat chunks with the peppers, the onions, the whole mushrooms, and an occasional cherry tomato thrown in for color. Set aside until later.

5:30 PM: For your salad you'll want spinach that is young and tender. The spinach must be carefully rinsed in a bowl of cool water, then dried with paper towels. Break the spinach leaves into small pieces. Mince the last onion and add it to the spinach. Slice several of the raw mushrooms and add them. In future spinach salads, you may want to try adding crumbled hard-boiled egg or croutons.

Cut the bacon into small pieces and fry over medium heat until cooked through. Add a tablespoon of Dijon mustard, a dash of Worcestershire sauce, and one fourth cup of white wine vinegar. Mix well and set aside until ready to serve.

6 PM: Barbecue the skewers over hot charcoal, turning them frequently and basting occasionally with the marinade. The trick is to have everything barbecued perfectly at the same time—the lamb should be browned on the outside, pink and succulent on the inside; the vegetables should be cooked but not burned. Lots of luck.

When the shish kebab is done, set the skewers to the side of the barbecue and dash back into the kitchen. Heat the bacon and vinegar over high heat until the mix starts to bubble, stir it, and pour it directly over the spinach. Serve it immediately along with the shish kebab.

And, finally, the tea. Take your pitcher of tea from the refrigerator. Strain out the tea leaves. Add some lemon and sugar and serve over ice cubes. You may have some trouble convincing the younger members of the family that this really is iced tea. But when you see the expressions on their faces, you'll have some inkling of how Richard Blechynden felt three quarters of a century ago on that day when he knew the enterprise was saved.

MENU 16

The Common Casserole
Green Goddess Salad
Blueberries in Sour Cream

The Special: When it was first invented by television executives, it was envisioned as an oasis in the vast wasteland. More than just a program that would depart from the routine, it was a distraction, a high spot designed to make you forget all those low spots.

Cooks can make use of the same theory. Every dinner, no matter how ordinary—especially, in fact, if it *is* ordinary—should have a Special. This is the dish that offers something unique, the dish that is served up with a small story, the dish that can take your mind off the rest of the meal. To put it another way: What does it matter if you've overcooked the chicken when you've had the wild rice flown in from your farm in Afghanistan? Tonight's Special is the salad dressing.

The Staples: Make sure that these are all on hand: salt, pepper, tarragon, dry mustard, cayenne pepper, eggs, oil for salad dressing, a lemon.

The Shopping List: One pound ground beef, one tin anchovy fillets, two large onions, two green peppers, one head romaine lettuce, one bunch scallions, chives, parsley, four ears corn, one pound noodles, two small cans tomato sauce, one half pound cheddar cheese, one small container sour cream, one container blueberries.

There are few dinners that are easier and less special than the common casserole. Whether it's macaroni and cheese, noodles and tuna fish, or something a little more complicated, like tonight's main dish, it should provide no great test of your growing culinary skills.

Your only test tonight will come with the salad dressing.

Prepare in Advance: The first thing you're going to make is mayonnaise. We all know that it's possible to begin with a jar of the ready-made stuff from the grocery shelf, but then your Special will not be all that special. And if we're going for the classic Green Goddess Dressing—the way it was first made and served in San Francisco's Palace Hotel—we're going to do it the right way, using an electric beater.

We'll need two egg yolks and no egg whites. Separating the yolk from the white requires a steady hand and a certain amount of practice. Break the egg into halves and carefully transfer the yolk from one half to the other, allowing the white to fall away.

When you have two yolks in a mixing bowl, add a pinch of dry mustard, a pinch of salt, and a few shakes of cayenne pepper. Beat this up for a couple of minutes and add just a few drops of salad oil. As you continue beating the egg mixture, add a tiny trickle of oil.

The mixture will thicken, and when this happens add a total of two cups of oil and three teaspoons of lemon juice in a slightly heavier but steady stream. Should the mayonnaise suddenly lose its consistency, add an ice cube and beat it into the mixture. Why this works I don't know, but it does. If it doesn't, start over.

To the two cups of mayonnaise, add the anchovy fillets, finely chopped, four scallions—both whites and greens—also finely chopped, a handful of chopped parsley, a small handful of chopped chives, and a large pinch of tarragon.

Store this in the refrigerator until ready to serve.

5 PM: And now for the easy part, the casserole. Start six quarts of water boiling in your largest pot. Add a small handful of salt.

Heat a splash of oil in a large frying pan over medium heat. Add the pound of ground beef, crumbled, and the onions, chopped. A couple of minutes later add the green peppers, cut into narrow strips. Finally, as the meat is browning, slice the kernels of corn from the ears with a sharp knife and add them. A couple of minutes after this, drain away the fat and salt and pepper to taste.

5:30 PM: Add the noodles to the boiling water. When cooking pasta, some cooks claim the water should be boiling fiercely. Others say it should be boiling merrily. I'm not sure what the difference is. However, if you put the noodles into the water slowly, you won't interrupt the mood, whether it be fierce or merry.

Cook the noodles a couple of minutes less than the box's recommended minimum time. Preheat the oven to 350 degrees.

5:40 PM: Drain the noodles and put them into a buttered baking dish. Add the meat-onion-pepper-corn mixture, the two cans of tomato sauce, and most of the cheddar cheese, grated. Mix this together and scatter the rest of the grated cheese across the top. Bake.

6:20 PM: Check the casserole to see whether the cheese is properly browned. Rinse the romaine lettuce, pat dry with paper towels, and break into small pieces. Add the Green Goddess Salad Dressing and explain, as you bring it out, the absolute necessity of using homemade mayonnaise.

The dinner, both ordinary and special, will be followed by blueberries served with a dollop of sour cream. If your dinner should still need a special touch—Special touch, that is—try adding a shot of maple syrup and a dash of cinnamon to the berries.

MENU 17

Tomatoes with Pesto
Lamb Shanks in Casserole
Poached Pears

After you've been cooking for a while, some dishes will acquire a definite sentimental value. It may be the first dinner that comes out perfectly. Or perhaps it will be a meal associated with a highly charged emotional event—a reunion of old friends, a family celebration, the first night your wife brings the boss home for dinner.

For me, this dish—an unlikely combination of lamb shanks, sweet potatoes, and green beans—has the strongest sentimental tug of them all, possibly because it's directly associated with one important aspect of the early marriage years: survival.

During those first years, when babies were arriving as rapidly as money was disappearing, there was one prime consideration when shopping for food: How much does it cost? If mankind had not invented macaroni, it is possible that this branch of the McGrady family would have been starved out. A big day was hamburger; the biggest day of all, an invitation to eat out.

I can remember window-shopping at butcher shops the way others might window-shop at jewelry stores. One day while window-shopping, I came upon a sign that said LAMB SHANKS. The other sign was a price tag, and it said *37 cents a pound.* Surely that was a typographical error. But no, thirty-seven cents was the correct price. It would be possible to buy almost three pounds of meat without breaking into a second dollar bill.

Buying a new cut of meat—whether it be shank of lamb or tongue of lark—always raises a question: What's the best way to cook it? Fortunately, at thirty-seven cents a pound, there was room for experimentation that year in the field of lamb shanks. Which is why I can guarantee that this recipe is one of the best things you can do with a lamb shank.

The Staples: Make sure that these are all on hand: garlic, lemons, olive oil, vegetable oil, sugar, salt, pepper, flour, paprika, vanilla.

The Shopping List: Three and a half pounds of lamb shanks, four large sweet potatoes, four large ripe tomatoes, four ripe pears, one pound of broad Italian green beans (either fresh or frozen), fresh basil (enough for two loosely packed cups of leaves), one half cup grated Parmesan cheese, one third cup of pine nuts or shelled walnuts.

Prepare in Advance: The pesto sauce for the tomatoes. Pesto is a basil sauce that goes well with many dishes. It adds a unique flavor to buttered noodles; it's just fine with string beans; it is often added to soups and salad dressings.

However, to use pesto to best advantage, serve it with sliced tomatoes. The fact that basil and tomatoes ripen simultaneously is one of nature's happy accidents. Incidentally, don't be alarmed if you have leftover sauce. Pesto keeps well and can be frozen with no great loss of flavor.

You'll be using the blender for this one. Rinse the basil leaves and pat dry. Add half a cup of olive oil, three cloves of chopped garlic, a dash of salt and pepper, the grated Parmesan cheese, and either the pine nuts or the shelled walnuts. Blend all this into a thick sauce and set aside.

Also Prepare in Advance: The dessert. Peel the pears and cut them into halves. Mix a cup of water with half a cup of sugar and boil. Add a capful of vanilla. Poach the pears over medium-low heat, stirring them once or twice. When they are soft, set them aside to cool.

4:45 PM: Preheat the oven to 350 degrees. If the green beans are frozen, take them out of the freezer to thaw.

Then, using a sharp knife, trim all excess fat away from the lamb shanks. Mix a handful of flour with a large pinch of paprika and some salt and pepper in a brown paper bag. Shake the lamb shanks in the bag until they are all heavily coated with the flour mixture.

Add a dash of vegetable oil to a large frying pan set over medium-high heat. Put the lamb shanks into the pan and turn them until they are well browned, then transfer them to an ovenproof casserole dish. Put the juice of two lemons into the frying pan, scrape up all the meat residues, and add to the casserole.

5 PM: Cover the casserole and place it in the preheated oven.

5:30 PM: Peel the sweet potatoes, cut them into thirds, and add them to the meat.

6 PM: A final addition to the pot: the green beans and the juice of a third lemon. Re-cover the casserole and return to the oven.

6:30 PM: Rinse and slice the tomatoes and serve them with the pesto. Check the casserole. The sweet potatoes should be soft, easily pierced by a fork. The lamb shanks should be tender, cooked to the point where the meat comes easily from the bone. Serve each helping with plenty of the vegetables and drippings.

Who was it who said, "You can't go home again?" Well, you can—but remember to bring money. The other day when I went back to cook this old survival favorite, I found the familiar sign LAMB SHANKS, beside a brand-new price tag: *$1.39 a pound.* It seems that even the cost of survival has gone up.

MENU 18

Fillet of Beef
Pickled Green Peppers
Potato Salad Supreme
Ripe Peaches and Pears
Vin Rosé

Nothing seems so inescapably American as the picnic. I've always slotted it right there beside Fourth-of-July parades and bleacher seats and cotton candy as an archetypically American experience.

Not so. The picnic—*pique-nique,* if you will—was invented by the French and perfected by the British, a people who manage to maintain a sense of elegance under the most adverse circumstances.

The starting point of a British picnic is the proper basket—a wicker valise, somewhat larger than an overnight bag, with room for the viands, not to mention the flatware, the monogrammed linen napkins, the silver salt and pepper shakers, the other essentials. I'm telling you, no one worries about ants on a British picnic—they worry about chipping the crystal.

While the British may tend to go a trifle overboard on a picnic, we Americans often go underboard, settling as often as not for sandwiches and six-packs. Today we're going to

hit a happy medium. Our at-home picnic is not exactly caviar, nor is it a bunch of baloney.

The Staples: Make sure that these are all on hand: peanut
oil, dry white wine, garlic, salt, pepper, cider vinegar, sugar,
mustard, butter.

The Shopping List: One rolled fillet of beef (five to seven
pounds), imported soy sauce, pumpernickel bread (two
loaves), three pounds new potatoes, one pound bacon, one
large Bermuda onion, one bunch parsley, one small jar pimientos, one small container of sour cream, one medium
cucumber, one head lettuce, five green peppers, ripe peaches and pears, one bottle of vin rosé.

Prepare the Day Before: Almost everything.
    Begin with the fillet of beef. Trim any excess fat. Put the
fillet into a baking dish with a marinade that consists of one
cup of soy sauce, half a cup of peanut oil, half a cup of
white wine, five chopped garlic cloves, and a handful of
chopped parsley. Every now and then during the next
twenty-four hours, turn the meat over.
    Now on to the potato salad. Begin by putting the un-
peeled potatoes into a potful of water and placing the pot
over high heat. Boil the potatoes until a fork passes through
them easily (generally about twenty minutes), and then
pour away the water and allow the potatoes to cool.
    Fry the bacon in a large pan over medium heat, turning
the bacon over so that it is cooked on both sides. When the
bacon is done, allow it to drain on paper towels, then chop
the bacon into postage-stamp-sized pieces and put them
into a large salad bowl.
    Add the Bermuda onion, chopped into small pieces. Peel
the cucumber, cut it into small cubes, and add that. Cut the

pimientos into small pieces and add them. And then, when the potatoes are cool enough to handle, peel them, cut them into chunks, and mix them with the other vegetables. Also add a small handful of chopped parsley and a generous amount of salt and pepper.

Then, the dressing. Potato salad goes well with a variety of dressings. Some prefer plain mayonnaise or mayonnaise diluted with a small amount of milk. Others opt for a basic oil-and-vinegar dressing. I prefer tossing it with a small container of sour cream mixed with a few spoons of vinegar.

And on the picnic, you'll have something just a little different—instantly pickled green peppers. You'll need a jar with a cap. Then cut the green peppers into halves and remove the seeds. Put the peppers under the broiler—cut side down—for just a few minutes, not to cook them through but just to heat them up. Take the peppers from the broiler, slice them into strips, and put them into the jar.

In a saucepan over medium-high heat place three quarters of a cup of cider vinegar, the same amount of water, and one quarter cup of sugar. Add two peeled garlic cloves, a dollop of oil, and a dash of salt and pepper. When the mixture reaches the boiling point, lower the heat and simmer for five or six minutes, then pour over the green pepper slices. Cap the jar and refrigerate overnight.

Prepare on the Day of the Picnic: The fillet. Preheat the oven to a hot 475 degrees. Put the fillet of beef into a roasting pan and cook for about thirty minutes for rare, longer if you want it well done. Every five or ten minutes while the beef is baking, baste it with the marinade. Wrap the roast in metal foil and allow it to cool completely before beginning your at-home picnic.

However, if you plan to do the road-show version of this

picnic, don't forget any of the essential ingredients. Remember to bring: a sharp knife for cutting thin slices off the fillet of beef, a butter knife for buttering and mustarding the pumpernickel bread, a cooler for the bottle of wine, not to mention a glass or two (and the often forgotten but absolutely indispensable corkscrew), and forks and plates for the potato salad and the pickled peppers. On second thought, you might want to look into one of those wicker picnic baskets; they're available anywhere in the British Isles.

MENU 19

Steak Tartare on Rye Rounds
Orange-and-Onion Salad
Carrot Cake with Cream Cheese Frosting

Today, a meal for the adventurous. Not that you must be adventurous to cook it; no, cooking this will be simple enough. The adventure comes with the eating. Each part of tonight's meal seems unlikely—an unlikely combination of ingredients that somehow work together just fine.

Courage! Life contains many gustatory rewards. For years I've enjoyed a tasty lime-flavored appetizer known as "seviche." And just the other day I learned it's made of raw fish. I'm sure I'll still enjoy it—if I ever try it again.

We each have limits. And I draw the line somewhere this side of chocolate-covered ants. But we should appreciate the fact that some of our early ancestors had more pioneering palates. What of the first humans to eat oysters? What explanation can there be for such courage? Did they lose early election bets? Were they incredibly adventurous? Or were they possibly very, very hungry?

The Staples: Make sure that these are all on hand: salt, pepper, Dijon mustard, Worcestershire sauce, cooking oil, olive oil, rosemary, granulated sugar, baking soda, cinnamon, vanilla, milk, eggs.

The Shopping List: Lean, high-quality beef (two pounds, ground twice by the butcher on the day you plan to use it), eggs, two large Bermuda onions, one small bottle capers, one bunch parsley, one loaf rye bread, three large oranges, one head romaine lettuce, one lemon, two pounds carrots, three cups cake flour, one cup chopped walnuts, one large package cream cheese, one pound powdered sugar.

One of the secrets in presenting tonight's meal is to avoid talking about it too much. Don't describe it; just serve it. Let the food explain itself.

Carrot cake, for example, sounds much too healthy. If kids hear the name, they may not give it a fair trial. And the reassuring truth: It's every bit as sweet and unhealthy and tasty as any other cake. And there is, surprisingly enough, no carrot flavor to the cake. The carrots serve to retain the moisture and give the cake a nice heft.

Prepare in Advance: The cake. Preheat the oven to 350 degrees. Using an electric beater, beat four eggs for several minutes and then mix in two cups of sugar and two thirds of a cup of oil. Mix in the cake flour, two teaspoons of baking soda, two tablespoons of cinnamon, one teaspoon of salt, and the chopped walnuts. Now the carrots—peel them and grate them until you have three cups of grated carrots. Mix this into the cake batter.

You should have enough cake batter to fill a 9-by-13-inch baking dish. Grease the baking dish with a little butter. Put the batter into the dish and the dish into the oven. The cake should be done in just half an hour. You can test it by jabbing it with a toothpick; if the toothpick comes out clean, the cake is done.

Set the cake aside while you make the frosting. Using the electric beater, mix the cream cheese with a teaspoon of vanilla, two tablespoons of milk, and the powdered sugar.

When the cake has cooled, spread this frosting over it.

6 PM: When you have finished the cake, you have completed all your cooking chores. You see, the primary difference between steak tartare and other steak dishes is this: Steak tartare is not cooked. That's right, you're about to feed your family raw meat, but not without some precautions. It should be a splendid piece of meat to begin with and then it should be ground—twice—as near the dinner hour as possible.

Put the ground meat into a mixing bowl. Peel and chop one of the Bermuda onions and add to the meat. Add the yolks of two eggs and half a small bottle of capers. Put in a large handful of minced parsley, several shakes of Worcestershire sauce, a dash of olive oil, a tablespoon of Dijon mustard, and a generous amount of freshly ground black pepper. Other popular additions: chopped anchovies, chives, a shot of cognac.

The steak tartare should be served in small portions, with good rye or pumpernickel bread and, once again, a minimum of discussion.

6:15 PM: The salad. Squeeze half an orange and mix the juice with a quarter cup of olive oil, the juice of half a lemon, a dash of salt, and a large pinch of rosemary. Peel the rest of the oranges and cut them into sections. Rinse and dry the romaine and break it into bite-sized pieces. Peel one Bermuda onion and slice it thinly. Add the dressing and serve.

It's possible that a dinner this far-out will not be greeted by wild applause. In fact, you may detect signs of rebellion. Not for the carrot cake, certainly—I've never heard anyone complain about that. And not for the salad, which tastes somewhat better than it sounds.

However, the serving of the Steak Tartare may be greeted

by some resistance and perhaps an occasional boo. What you do then is simple enough. You form the Steak Tartare into flat patties and you put them into a frying pan over medium heat and you turn them once and what you will have then are the world's fanciest hamburgers.

MENU 20

Chilled Tomato Soup
Wheat Salad
Japanese Vegetable Pancakes
Fruit and Cheese Tray

Consider the poor vegetarian. While the rest of the gang is ordering a second martini, he's fantasizing about a carrot juice cocktail with just a soupçon of ... oh ... sauerkraut squeezings. While you're polishing off a juicy steak and then lighting up a postprandial cigar, he's getting suited up for his evening jog. Ah, never to know the thrill of a Big Mac, a hot dog, a slab of roast beef. ... I tell you, there's something definitely un-American about the common garden-variety vegetarian.

The only trouble with the vegetarian way of life, it's at least mildly contagious. Several years ago, strictly as an economy measure, our family tried one meatless meal a week. We found we could do very nicely with an omelet or a soufflé on that one night. And a cheese casserole worked pretty well on another night. Every now and then there was an all-salad night. The way things now stand, a month can go by before we sink our teeth into anything more profound than a chicken.

This happens to be my favorite meatless meal. Try it just
for the fun of it. But be forewarned: Once you start, there's
no telling where it will lead.

The Staples: Make sure that these are all on hand: olive oil,
salt, pepper, eggs, unbleached flour, soy sauce, garlic.

The Shopping List: Four large ripe tomatoes, three large
Bermuda onions, dill (preferably fresh), one box of wheat
pilaf (you may have to visit the health food store for this),
one large potato, one bunch parsley, scallions, three lemons,
one head cabbage, four carrots, two green peppers, cucumber, celery, whole wheat flour, evaporated milk (thirteen-
ounce can), small container sour cream, various cheeses and
fruits in season.

Prepare in Advance: The tomato soup. Peel the ripe tomatoes. The way to do this: Dip them in boiling water for less
than a minute. The skin will fall away easily with a little
prodding from a paring knife. Slice the peeled tomatoes and
put them into a saucepan over medium heat. Add one large
onion, chopped; two cloves of garlic, minced; a large pinch
of dill, minced; a potato, peeled and sliced thinly; a generous amount of salt; and freshly ground pepper. Set the heat
to low, cover the pot, and simmer the soup until the potato
is cooked through—fifteen to twenty minutes.

Pour the soup into an electric blender and mix it until it
is smooth. Stir in the sour cream and put the mixture into
the refrigerator to cool.

Also Prepare in Advance: The wheat salad. Wheat pilaf
can be found in some supermarkets and most health food
stores. Put one cup of wheat pilaf into a bowl. Boil two cups
of water over high heat and add that to the pilaf. The pilaf

will absorb the water in less than an hour. When it is cool, add one green pepper, chopped fine. Peel and grate two large carrots and add them. Peel a cucumber, cut it into tiny pieces, and add that. Peel and chop an onion and add that.

And now the seasonings. Add a large handful of chopped parsley, a pinch of salt, and pepper to taste. And then a salad dressing consisting of a third of a cup of freshly squeezed lemon juice and the same amount of olive oil.

Allow the salad to cool before you serve it. Always serve this salad with a word of warning: This salad can be habit forming. It undoubtedly has something to do with the absence of whole grains in our diet, but I've seen sophisticated and very picky eaters work their way through three helpings, apologizing all the while, and then ask for a fourth.

5:45 PM: All that remains: The Japanese vegetable pancakes. Most of the cooking done in an Oriental kitchen seems to be slicing-and-dicing work.

Using a sharp knife, shred half a head of cabbage, slicing it first one way and then the other. Chop two peeled carrots as fine as possible. Peel and chop the last onion. Chop four of the celery stalks without their leaves. Cut a green pepper into small bits.

Beat one egg for a few minutes and then mix in the can of evaporated milk. Stir in a cup of whole wheat flour and a cup of unbleached white flour. Add a teaspoon of salt and all the chopped vegetables. Chances are the batter will be a little thick at this point. If so, add a splash of water—or maybe two splashes—until the batter is more liquid than solid.

Heat a large frying pan or a griddle over medium heat and add a dab of butter or a splash of cooking oil. Using a soup ladle, pour small puddles of the batter onto the pan. Cook for three or four minutes and then take a peek; when the pancakes start to brown on one side, flip them over and cook until they are browned on both sides.

Don't worry about leftovers—they're excellent served cold the following day.

6:30 PM: Begin with the cold tomato soup, garnished with sprigs of dill or some chopped cucumber.

Follow with the wheat pilaf salad, served on a bed of lettuce or cabbage leaves. Follow that with the vegetable pancakes, served with soy sauce. (*Danger!* No syrup.)

Finally, follow with a selection of fruit and cheese.

MENU 21

Corned Beef and Cabbage Dinner
Beer
Irish Coffee

During recent years, this country's major new development in the field of humor has been the ethnic joke. A single example should suffice.

Q: What do you think of an IQ of 184?

A: That's *very* impressive!

Q: For the whole country of _____?

You can, of course, fill in the blank space with the name of any country. And that's the beauty of ethnic humor; all countries can be maligned equally.

However, not too long ago I heard this following joke and, as you might imagine, had difficulty believing my ears.

The question: "What's a seven-course banquet in Ireland?" The answer: "A boiled potato and a six-pack."

Well, talk about your tawdry attempts to garner cheap laughs! It is one thing to make fun of other nationalities. But when they start in after the Irish, they are going too far. This deplorable trend must cease at once. And besides, they don't even have it right. This is the way it should have gone:

Q: What's a thirteen-course meal in Ireland?

A: A piece of corned beef, a slab of cabbage, a few boiled potatoes, some turnips, Irish coffee, and a six-pack.

Tonight, an Irish banquet.

The Staples: Make sure that these are all on hand: whiskey (Irish, if possible), mustard, horseradish, butter, coffee, sugar, salt, cloves, peppercorns, beer.

The Shopping List: Corned beef (four to five pounds), one bunch of parsley, two pounds of potatoes (preferably small ones), one pound of carrots, two pounds of turnips and/or parsnips, three large onions, one large head of cabbage, a small container of cream.

You can, if you wish, make your own corned beef from scratch, buying a large brisket of beef and refrigerating it in a gallon of corning solution for just less than a month. However, keeping all this in the refrigerator may not endear you to the rest of the family, so why don't we begin by just buying a piece of previously corned beef?

Cooking this piece of meat is going to require a good amount of time, anywhere from three to four hours, depending on the weight of the meat, so plan on beginning fairly early in the day.

2:30 PM: Put the corned beef into a deep, heavy pot and cover it with cold water. Turn the heat to high. When the water comes to a boil, reduce the heat to low and just keep the water simmering. At this time you can add a pinch of cloves, the same amount of peppercorns, and the onions chopped fine.

5:30 PM: Peel the turnips and/or parsnips but do not slice them. Add them to the pot.

5:45 PM: Now add the carrots, peeled but not sliced. When the carrots are in the pot, peel the potatoes.

6 PM: Add the potatoes. At this point, you are doubtless wondering how you can be sure that all these various ingredients—and we haven't even come to the cabbage—are going to be done at precisely the same time. Well, you can't be sure. And in fact, if it happens that it works out that way, everything cooked properly at the same exact moment, this may be your day to invest in the stock market.

But this last half hour, you'll be doing a lot of testing, jabbing one of those two-pronged forks here and there. When the fork passes easily through the center of the meat, it is done. At this time, if the vegetables have not completed their cooking, remove the corned beef from the pot, wrap it in metal foil, and return it for a final hot bath just before serving it.

6:10 PM: Cut the head of cabbage in half and slice away the core. Then cut the halves into wedges and add them to the pot. The cabbage should be tender in fifteen to twenty minutes.

Meanwhile, if any of the vegetables have become tender, they can be removed from the pot and held aside until the final moment. However, at 6:25, all the ingredients should be back in the pot.

6:30 PM: Slice the corned beef across the grain into moderately thin slices and arrange them on the center of a serving platter. Surround them with the vegetables and allow butter to melt over the lot. Add a sprinkling of chopped parsley and serve in the company of mustard and horseradish. Then go to the refrigerator and fetch the next six courses.

After dinner serve the Irish coffee—two ounces of good whiskey, a teaspoon of sugar, and strong coffee, all of it topped with cream. According to James Joyce, the cream should be poured "slowly in circular motion. Allow cream to float on top of coffee. Do not stir again. Excellent for after-dinner conversation."

Incidentally, don't be concerned if there are leftovers. The following morning you will chop up the corned beef and add it to chopped onions and chopped potatoes. You will fry until it is browned on all sides and you will serve this corned beef hash with ketchup, salt, and pepper. While most will dig into the hash, some will have two Alka-Seltzers, which is the kind of breakfast that people often have on the morning after a major banquet.

MENU 22

Vichyssoise

Artichokes

Roast Loin of Pork

Rice Salad

Coffee with Rum

Some meals are particularly right for summer—iced drinks, large salads, cold meats, corn on the cob, and so forth. And there are meals one associates with winter—steaming soups, large roasts, heaps of potatoes.

But what do you do while the seasons are changing? How do you plan a dinner when you're subjected to the uncertainties of autumn or the vagaries of spring, those awkward days when the weather forecasters are using words like "variable" and "mixed" and "partially"?

Well, each dish tonight has one quality in common. No, two qualities. In the first place, each dish tastes good. Second, each dish tastes good whether it's served ice cold or piping hot or, for that matter, lukewarm.

Tonight, the all-temperature dinner.

The Staples: Make sure that these are all on hand: olive oil, butter, lemons, soy sauce, mayonnaise, salt, pepper, tarragon, thyme, garlic, curry powder, coffee, rum, milk, sherry.

The Shopping List: One five- to six-pound loin of pork (have your butcher bone it and tie it), small jar of currant jelly, rice, one green pepper, one small can of water chestnuts, four leeks, five artichokes, one bunch scallions, one medium onion, one cucumber, three pounds potatoes, two cups light cream, two small cans chicken broth, chives, parsley.

Let's assume that the weather forecaster is waffling today. While tonight's meal can be reheated and served hot, it is normally—and to best advantage—served cold, in which case the entire meal should be prepared in advance.

Beginning with the Vichyssoise: Wash the leeks carefully under cool running water. (*Danger!* Very carefully. For some reason, leeks attract more sand than your average beach.)

Slice the whites of the leeks—only the whites—and put these into a heavy pot with half a stick of butter. Add the onion, peeled and chopped. Cook over medium heat for five to ten minutes, until the onion begins to turn translucent. Peel the potatoes, slice them, and add the slices to the pot. Also add the cans of chicken broth. Bring all this to a boil, then immediately reduce the heat to low. Simmer for somewhat less than an hour.

When the mixture has cooled, run it through the blender. What you have now might be called vichyssoise concentrate. Store it in the refrigerator and, just before serving, mix in one and a half cups of light cream. If the soup still seems too thick, it can be thinned with chicken broth, light cream, or milk. Each serving—whether it be hot or cold—should be topped with freshly ground pepper and a scattering of chopped chives.

Next, the Artichokes: There should be directions for eating, not cooking, artichokes. Cut off the stems and stand the artichokes up on their bottoms in a pot of water over medium-high heat. Cook until tender—oh, forty-five minutes or slightly more. Then turn them upside down to drain. Serve them with a dip and with a separate plate for discarded leaves.

Remove one leaf at a time and dip the meaty end of the leaf into a sauce and scrape that portion away with your teeth. As you work your way into the plant, you will be able to eat larger portions of the leaves. The inner leaves and the feathery portion above the artichoke heart should be removed and discarded. The heart is then cut into small pieces, dipped, and eaten.

If the artichoke is to be served hot, I like a dip of melted butter with a squeeze of lemon. If cold, try mayonnaise with a dash of curry powder.

Moving Right Along to the Loin of Pork: The pork loin is marinated overnight in half a cup of olive oil, half a cup of sherry, one fourth cup of soy sauce, a pinch of thyme, and three cloves of garlic, chopped. Turn the meat over several times in the marinade.

Preheat the oven to 325 degrees. Allow plenty of roasting time—about thirty minutes for each pound of pork. While the roast is cooking, baste it several times with marinade.

Heat the currant jelly in a small saucepan over medium-high heat until it bubbles. Add four tablespoons of marinade and cook for a few more minutes. Coat the pork with the mixture when the cooking is complete.

You can then—depending on your mood or the mood of

the weather—serve it hot (good), cold (better), or warm (best).

Now, the Rice Salad: Cook one cup of dry rice according to the directions on the box. Add the green pepper, chopped fine; one cucumber, chopped; the small can of water chestnuts, sliced; and a bunch of scallions, chopped.

Make a salad dressing from one third cup of olive oil, three tablespoons of lemon juice, salt and pepper, a large pinch of minced parsley, and a small pinch of tarragon. Toss with the rice mixture.

And, Finally, the Coffee with Rum: You mix each cup of coffee with a jigger of rum and two jiggers of cream and serve it hot, cold, or whatever.

MENU 23

Steak

Spuds

Peas

Pie

This one is for the he-man, the all-American male, that ma-cho guy who balks whenever something a little exotic is recommended—say, a cold soup, a sauce with more than one spice, or any of those "Frenchified" dishes.

Tonight, the no-frills meal. Nothing too fancy, nothing too foreign, nothing a normal American can't pronounce, spell, or eat. Tonight, it's back to the basics, the kind of meal you can sling together for a bunch of the guys between football games, the kind of meal you can serve up with a bottle of ketchup and a simple announcement: "It's chow time."

The Staples: Make sure that these are all on hand: butter, salt, coarsely ground pepper, ketchup (optional), cooking oil, white sugar, brown sugar, flour, cinnamon, nutmeg.

The Shopping List: Four pounds of boneless steak (sirloin or club, about an inch in thickness), six large Idaho potatoes, one small container sour cream, chives, peas (three cups of fresh peas, shelled, or two packages of frozen peas), Boston lettuce (one small head), one bunch parsley, one bunch scallions, six cooking apples (large, tart), frozen piecrust, one half pound cheddar cheese.

We begin with the pie. It's possible, of course, to make the piecrust from scratch, but there's no way you're going to explain *that* to the guys. So let's start with frozen piecrusts. (*Caution:* Check thawing instructions on the package.)

4:30 PM: Preheat the oven to 450 degrees. In a large bowl, mix together half a cup of white sugar, half a cup of brown sugar, a large pinch of ground cinnamon, a small pinch of nutmeg, and a tiny pinch of salt. Add two tablespoons of flour.

Now peel the apples and cut away the cores. Slice the apples and add the slices to the bowl. Stir.

Spread small dots of butter—a couple of tablespoons in all—over the base of the pie. Add the apple mixture and spread the upper crust over the heaped fruit. Using a sharp knife, poke several steam holes in the upper crust.

4:50 PM: Place the pie in the hot oven.

5:10 PM: Lower the oven heat from 450 degrees to 375 degrees.

5:30 PM: Now, on to the steak. There are some people who would call this kind of meat "steak *au poivre,*" but you don't have to be one of them. Using the heel of your hand, press fresh coarsely ground black pepper into both sides of the steak. Leave the meat at room temperature until you're ready to cook it.

5:40 PM: Piecrust should be brown and bubbly. If so, remove the pie from the oven. If not, give it a few more minutes.

Rinse the potatoes well, then roll them in a small amount of cooking oil until they are evenly coated. Salt the potato skins and put the potatoes on a rack in the oven. They should be done in forty-five minutes to an hour.

5:50 PM: Now turn your attention to the peas. Although you're going to cook the peas in the French style, there's no need to tell the fellows about this.

Peas can be cooked in four or five minutes, but we'll simmer—not boil—them about thirty minutes. Put half a cup of water in a heavy saucepan over medium-high heat. Add the peas, either fresh or frozen. Rinse, peel, and chop the scallions—both green and white portions—and add them. Rinse the small head of lettuce, slice it into strips, and add these. Also add a small handful of parsley, chopped, and some salt and pepper. Just before the mixture comes to a boil, turn the heat very low. Cover the pot and allow to simmer. (*Caution:* Check occasionally to make sure the water hasn't boiled away.)

6:10 PM: We're ready now to pan-broil the steak. Since this can be a smoky business, we're going to cut most of the fat away from the meat.

Heat a large, heavy skillet over high heat. When the skillet is very hot, add the meat. Brown the steak quickly on one side. This should take a minute or less. Turn the steak over and brown the other side. Lower the heat to medium and cook the steak six to eight additional minutes. Then flip it back over for six to eight minutes more on the first side.

6:30 PM: The peas should be tender now, ready to serve at any time. When a fork passes easily into the potatoes, they're ready. Serve them up with sour cream and chopped chives. Using a sharp knife, cut into the center of the steak and test that for doneness. Naturally, you'll want to serve this with no embellishments, no fancy sauces—maybe just that bottle of ketchup—and after that, it's every man for himself.

You may have a bad moment or two later on as you're dishing up the apple pie with a nice slab of cheddar. This may raise an eyebrow or two. But you can do what any real man would do. Say your wife made it.

MENU 24

Roast Turkey
Mashed Potatoes
Green Beans Parmesan
Ice Cream

Turkey? What's the occasion? Aha, that's the whole problem with turkey. It's one of those unfortunate dishes—like fruitcake (Christmas), baked ham (Easter)—that are so solidly linked to a specific holiday that we have trouble imagining them, or cooking them, any other time of the year.

I'm not saying you can't find turkey during the rest of the year. But you have to look for it. And where you generally find it, covered with mayo, is nestled between the bacon and the lettuce in your basic club sandwich.

This is a shame. Turkey has many virtues other than just tasting good. Usually, there is enough meat on a single bird to feed both your mob and a full set of visiting in-laws. Then, too, it's the leftover champ of the Free World—useful for soups, gravies, salads, and hashes. And there's always enough to fit nicely between the lettuce and the bacon in the next day's club sandwich.

Turkey. What's the occasion? Maybe the turkey itself should be the occasion.

The Staples: Make sure that these are all on hand: garlic, olive oil, wine vinegar, salt, pepper, butter, paprika.

The Shopping List: One turkey (ten pounds will do nicely), four pounds of potatoes, one small package of cream cheese, three onions, one and a half pounds of string beans, one lemon, one orange, four ounces of grated Parmesan cheese, one quart of ice cream.

There are several distinct advantages to preparing this un-Thansgiving turkey. In the first place, you don't have to cook all the side dishes that people consider part of the holiday tradition. Second, you don't have to follow the traditional baking methods that too often produce a bird just a bit on the dry side.

3 PM: Preheat the oven to 400 degrees. Today we're going to be using a Dutch oven; that's the large baking dish with the tight cover that fits into the oven. If you can't locate one of those, it's possible to get by with a deep baking dish and a tight covering of metal foil.

As the oven heats up, prepare the paste that you're going to smear over the turkey. Mince three cloves of garlic. Add a large pinch of paprika, a generous amount of salt and pepper, and enough freshly squeezed lemon juice to form a paste. Paint this over the surface of the bird.

Peel two medium-sized onions and cut them into small chunks. Place these in the turkey cavity. Slice the orange into thin slices and lay these slices over the entire surface of the turkey.

At this point, if your wife happens to wander into the kitchen, she may make an observation: "That's no way to cook a turkey!" Don't listen. It may not be the standard way to cook a turkey, but in some families it has become that.

3:15 PM: Put the turkey into the Dutch oven and make sure the cover is tight. Place the pot in the preheated oven.

4:15 PM: Lower the oven temperature to 350 degrees. Remove the cover (or metal foil) and, every twenty minutes or so, baste the bird with its own juices.

5:15 PM: Remove the orange slices from the body of the turkey. Add a slight dusting of paprika. Return the bird to the oven for its third and final hour of baking. Continue to baste it periodically with the pan juices.

5:30 PM: Cut the tips from the green beans and then slice the beans lengthwise. (Cutting off tips of beans is one of the world's dullest tasks, and you may want to con one of the kids into doing it.) Peel one small onion and chop it fine. Add a clove of garlic, minced, the grated Parmesan cheese, four tablespoons of olive oil, two tablespoons of wine vinegar, and a pinch of salt and pepper. Set this aside until the beans are cooked.

5:45 PM: Start a large pot of water boiling for the potatoes and a small pot of water for the string beans. Then peel the potatoes.

6:10 PM: Drop the potatoes into boiling water and boil them until a fork passes through them easily—usually about twenty minutes. Drop the string beans into a smaller pot and boil for just a few minutes, until they are tender. Drain the water away from the beans and add the Parmesan mixture; keep warm over low heat until ready to serve.

6:15 PM: Check the turkey for doneness. If the drumsticks seem loose in their sockets, the bird is cooked through. A second test: Jab a sharp knife into the turkey thigh; if the liquid that escapes is yellowish or clear, the bird is well done. If it's still pink, more cooking time is required.

6:30 PM: Remove the potatoes from the boiling water and mash with an electric beater. Cut a stick of butter into small pieces and add these to the hot potatoes along with the small package of cream cheese. Beat until smooth and add salt and pepper to taste.

Much has been written about the proper way to carve a turkey. I have read these instructions every year, and I have never yet managed to summon up the requisite surgical dexterity. You will soon discover that any method that separates the meat from the rest of the turkey will be just fine with the family.

MENU 25

Chicken Curry
Rice
Mangoes
Darjeeling Tea

Now it may happen that you are entertaining a visitor from a foreign country. And it may be that you have learned to make a dish from this person's native land. And perhaps, in order to make your guest feel at home, you are contemplating the preparation of a meal from his place of birth.

Don't do it. Repeat: Do not do it. Do not make pasta for an Italian, do not make borscht for a Russian, and never make curry for an Indian. Your aim would doubtless be a noble one, the easing of your guest's homesickness. But try to look at the situation this way: Better homesick than just plain sick.

The Staples: Make sure that these are all on hand: salt, pepper, flour, lemon, butter, vegetable oil, rice, garlic. *And these special seasonings:* cumin, coriander, turmeric, fenugreek, chili powder (or, if you want to take the coward's way out: just curry powder).

The Shopping List: Three pounds of boned chicken breasts, one coconut (fresh, if available), one pineapple (fresh, if possible), two fresh mangoes, one green apple, one bunch scallions, one green pepper, two large onions, three stalks celery, one half pound bacon, one jar of chutney, one small container yogurt (plain), one can chicken broth, Darjeeling tea.

Curry, in this country, can often be translated as "leftovers." The common technique is to mix any leftover meat with some chopped onion, some rice, and a slug of curry powder.

Well, tonight we'll hope to do better than that. And the first improvement will be to blend our own seasonings. Thus the list of strange-sounding herbs and spices above. There may be some people who believe that curry powder comes from the curry bush or perhaps the curry nut; the truth is that it is a blend of other seasonings—as few as five, as many as thirty. Most Indian cooks would insist on the customized version, not the assembly-line model. The entire list can be replaced by one small jar of curry powder, but at least give it a try this way.

Prepare in Advance: The curry. The curry itself can be made a day ahead of time or just before it's served. Allow yourself slightly more than an hour to put it together.

Begin with the boned chicken breasts. Using a sharp knife, cut them into bite-sized pieces. Dust each piece with flour. The easiest way to do this: Put some flour into a brown paper bag, add the chicken pieces, and shake them up.

Place half a stick of butter and a splash of vegetable oil in a large frying pan over medium heat. When the butter is melted, add the chicken pieces—as many as you can handle conveniently. Cook them about four minutes on each side and then transfer them to another bowl.

Using the same pan, adding more butter and oil as necessary, put in the onions, peeled and chopped; the green pepper, seeded and chopped; the celery stalks, chopped; two cloves of garlic, peeled and minced; and the green apple, peeled and cored and chopped. Cook over medium heat until they are all cooked soft.

Add the spices: a generous amount of freshly ground pepper; a pinch of salt; a tablespoon of coriander, another of cumin, and one of turmeric; half a teaspoon of fenugreek and the same amount of chili powder. (Or, if you're taking the easy way out, two to three tablespoons of curry powder—let your taste guide you.) Now add the chicken broth and bring the mixture to a boil. Lower the heat, stir in the plain yogurt, and simmer for fifteen minutes, stirring occasionally.

Add the chicken pieces, along with the juice of a lemon, and continue to simmer over low heat for the next thirty minutes. This can be either served immediately or reheated and used later.

6 PM: Cook one cup of dry rice, according to the directions on the box. Simmer the curry over low heat. During the cooking time, you will be putting together half a dozen different condiments that are to be served on small plates with the curry. These small dishes, the sideshows to the main event, are passed to the diners, who take as much or as little as they see fit.

Begin by frying the bacon in a large frying pan over medium heat. Cook on both sides, drain the fat away on paper towels, and crumble the bacon into small bits.

If you have located a fresh coconut, you can begin by adding a healthy shot of the coconut milk to the curry itself. Then grate enough of the coconut meat to fill one of the small plates. If you've found a fresh pineapple, cut part of it into chunks and use that as one of the side dishes.

Chop up the scallions—both whites and greens—and put them onto a separate plate. And, most important of all: the chutney. Serve that as a side dish on its own plate.

Other popular condiments in this country include raisins, nuts, and chopped hard-boiled eggs. In India they like chopped bananas, chopped onions and tomatoes served in milk, and diced cucumbers in yogurt.

And after all this, something cooling and appropriate——Darjeeling tea, served with sliced mangoes.

MENU 26

Spanakopita (Spinach Pie)
Greek Salad
Lamb Chops (Optional)
Greek Coffee

Every cook has one favorite dish. This is the one you wheel out for employers, in-laws, visiting philanthropists, and your wife's former flame. The requirements? It should look sensational when it's brought to the table; the first bite should melt in your mouth while jarring your taste buds right out of their slumber; later, when everyone is loosening a belt, the dish should be the main topic of conversation.

In our house that dish is . . . spinach pie. But that sounds so mundane, so humdrum. Well, the Greeks have a word for it: "Spanakopita." And that word, translated accurately into contemporary English, means "SuperDish."

Whenever it's served, you can almost choreograph the reactions. There's the first bite: "Mmmmm, what's this?" The second bite: "Hey, what *is* this?" By the third bite, they should be making room for a second helping, and by the fourth bite, they'll be begging for the recipe. Here it is.

The Staples: Make sure these are on hand: eggs, salt, pepper, oregano, rosemary, garlic, lemons, mustard, olive oil, sugar.

The Shopping List: Lamb chops (one per person), two pounds of feta cheese, one pound of filo dough (thin sheets, available in food specialty shops), two pounds spinach (fresh, if possible), two large onions, one pound butter, one head of lettuce, one cucumber, one pound cherry tomatoes, olives, one green pepper, Turkish or Greek coffee.

Since spinach pie is the most complicated dish we've undertaken so far, the rest of tonight's meal has been kept simple. Some preliminary warnings. You will absolutely need a pastry brush to spread butter over the thin sheets of dough. Second, a visit to a food specialty shop will be a must. There is no good substitute for feta cheese, and both main dishes require it. And the ultrathin sheets of filo dough are also a necessity; I have made the attempt, and I can now report there is no known way for human beings to make filo dough from scratch.

4:15 PM: Melt a large chunk of butter—three or four tablespoons—in a frying pan over medium heat. Add an onion, chopped fine, and one clove of garlic, minced. Cook until the onions are softened.

Now turn your attention to the fresh spinach. (If you are using frozen spinach, thaw completely and drain.) Rinse the fresh spinach several times in a pot of cool water. Dry it with paper towels, chop it fine, and add it to the onions. Then add salt, pepper, a large pinch of oregano, and half that much rosemary.

4:50 PM: Separate half a dozen eggs, putting the yolks into one bowl and the whites into another. Using a hand mixer, beat the egg yolks for a few minutes and then blend in one pound of feta cheese, crumbled. Stir in the spinach mixture. Finally, beat the egg whites until they are stiff and carefully fold them into the rest of the pie filling.

5:10 PM: Preheat the oven to 350 degrees. Melt half a pound of butter in a small saucepan over low heat. *(Danger!* Take it away from the heat before it turns brown.) Carefully unroll the filo dough—carefully because the sheets are not much thicker than tracing paper.

Using the pastry brush, paint the bottom of a rectangular baking dish—9 by 13 inches would be fine—with melted butter. Lay a single sheet of filo dough over the pan and brush butter on the dough. Lay another sheet over that. Butter it. And another. And so on until you have perhaps ten sheets of dough. Then spoon in the spinach mixture and cover it with another sheet of dough. Butter that one. Repeat until you have used up the filo. Then butter the top. Bake the pie between fifty minutes and an hour, using your eye for judgment.

5:30 PM: Now for the Greek Salad. Rinse and dry the head of lettuce and break it into small pieces. Cut the rest of the feta cheese into small chunks and add that, along with the cherry tomatoes, a sliced onion, a sliced cucumber, a sliced green pepper, and a large handful of olives. Then make a simple salad dressing—one part lemon juice, three parts olive oil, a minced clove of garlic, a touch of mustard, salt, and pepper. Pour the dressing over the salad just before serving.

6 PM: There are two reasons for listing the lamb chops as optional. You might check the price—okay, that's one reason. Second, the dinner doesn't really require them. Personally, I'd replace the chops with a Greek specialty—say a can of stuffed grape leaves, chilled and served with lemon wedges.

However, if you're going with the chops, rub each one with a peeled clove of garlic and some salt and pepper. Broil them about four inches from the flame. If the chops are reasonably thick, you should be able to broil them in about five or six minutes a side.

6:30 PM: A dinner this rich doesn't really require dessert. Let 'em eat fruit! Moreover, Greek coffee is rich enough to satisfy most dessert tastes. In two cups of water, add six teaspoons of the highly pulverized Greek or Turkish coffee and an equal amount of sugar. Let the coffee come to a boil and pour the froth into demitasse cups. Put the coffee on for another quick boil and fill the cups with more froth. Do not stir.

MENU 27

Herbed Chicken
Parsleyed Rice Casserole
Tossed Greens
Pound Cake

Well, gang, here we are at the halfway mark. The faithful reader has now cooked twenty-six complete meals—working his way slowly from spaghetti to spanakopita—and there are just twenty-six meals to go. The moment seems right for a little pep talk, a little halftime chat with the guys in the locker room.

We can do it, gang. Oh, I know it hasn't been easy. I know the curry wasn't perfect, and I heard what happened when you tried to light up the Steak Diane. And, hey, I'm sorry about the family's reaction when they discovered that Steak Tartare meant raw meat. But, listen, no one ever told you that this was going to be easy, that life is just a bowl of Chicken Teriyaki.

As we begin the second half, I don't want to see anyone letting up. When the going gets tough, the tough get going. And remember what lies off there in the distance: Chicken Kiev, Oysters Rockefeller, Crepes Suzette. Come on, gang, let's win this one for the little lady!

The Staples: Make sure that these are all on hand: flour, salt, pepper, tarragon, lemons, butter, garlic, dill, milk, double-acting baking powder, lemon extract, vanilla, sugar, vinegar, salad oil.

The Shopping List: Four to five pounds of broiling chicken (cut into small pieces), one bunch parsley, one bunch chives, a dozen eggs, one large onion, one head lettuce, rice, cake flour, a small container of sour cream.

The main difficulty tonight is going to be an overcrowded oven; three of the dishes require the use of an oven. Two of them—the chicken and the rice—can be baked simultaneously. But the cake should be baked in advance.

Prepare in Advance: The pound cake. Preheat the oven to 325 degrees. Allow three sticks of butter to soften outside the refrigerator.

We're going to have to use an electric beater on this one. Cut the butter into pieces and add a cup of sugar. Beat the butter and sugar together and then add two more cups of sugar, one cup at a time. Beat together until they form a mixture that is light and fluffy.

You'll be using eight eggs for the cake. Add the eggs to the mixture one at a time, beating each egg in before going on to the next.

In another bowl, stir together four cups of cake flour with a large pinch of salt and four level teaspoons of double-acting baking powder. Stir this into the other mixture along with the sour cream, a teaspoon of lemon extract, and a teaspoon of vanilla. Stir this together just until it is well mixed.

Take two 9-by-5-inch loaf pans (the kind that would be used for bread) and butter them. The easiest way to do this is to take a tiny piece of paper towel, dip it into soft butter, and rub this over the inside of the loaf pan. Dust the buttered surface with cake flour and then pour in the batter until each pan is three quarters filled.

The baking time may vary somewhat according to the thickness of the cake. Bake it for an hour and then test it for doneness. The way to do this: Insert a toothpick into the center of the cake; if it comes out clean, the cake is ready. After about fifteen minutes, remove the cake from the pan.

The rest of tonight's dinner will present no great problem to the halftime veteran. By now we all realize there's no great trick to cooking chicken, whether you broil it or bake it. This is all you really need to know about baking chicken: Use plenty of butter, plenty of lemon, and almost any spice on the shelf—rosemary, tarragon, marjoram, or thyme.

5 PM: Preheat the oven to 275 degrees. Begin with a brown paper bag. Into the bag put a cup of regular flour; a small handful of tarragon, either fresh or dried; half a bunch of parsley, chopped fine; a handful of chives, also chopped fine; and a generous amount of salt and pepper. Now add the chicken, cut into small pieces. Shake the bag until all the chicken pieces are coated with the flour and seasonings.

Lay the chicken in a shallow baking dish and dot each piece with butter. Sprinkle lemon juice over all and cover with metal foil. Place in the oven. Every twenty minutes or so, spoon the drippings over the chicken.

5:15 PM: Cook one cup of dry rice according to the directions on the box. In a separate frying pan, melt a chunk of butter over medium heat. Add one large onion, chopped, and cook until soft.

When the rice is ready, stir in the onion, the rest of the parsley, chopped fine, two beaten eggs, and half a cup of milk. Butter an ovenproof casserole dish and put the rice mixture into it.

5:50 PM: Increase the oven heat to 325 degrees. Remove the foil from the chicken. Put the rice casserole onto another oven shelf.

6:15 PM: All that remains is to put together a little salad. Tonight it will be just a head of lettuce, rinsed, dried with a paper towel, and broken into bite-sized pieces. Add a simple dressing—one part vinegar, four parts oil, a little minced garlic, a dash of dill, and some salt and pepper.

6:30 PM: All right, gang, time's up. You know what you've got to do now. You've got to get the chicken and the rice from the oven. You've got to pour the dressing over the salad. The rest of it? Hey, this one's going to be a piece of cake.

MENU 28

Beef Bourguignon
Garlic Bread
Red Wine
Sliced Oranges in Grand Marnier

Thursday was stew night. Nothing was ever spelled out, nothing written on the calendar, but most Thursdays of my boyhood wound up with a steaming bowl of stew. Maybe my mother was using up the remnants of the Monday shopping trip; perhaps she was just taking a breather before the big weekend meals. Whatever the reason, if we sat down to a stew, we knew it must be Thursday.

Not that there was anything wrong with my mother's stew. It's just that stew, through the ages, has suffered from bad public relations. From the beginning, the word "stew" has had unfortunate connotations. Originally it meant a hothouse, then a brothel, then a prostitute. Even today a man in trouble is said to be "in a stew."

Which explains why you can go into the world's fanciest restaurants and never find a menu with the word "stew." In time, as memories of my mother's stew faded, I occasionally went into a fancy restaurant. It was there that I first ordered Beef Bourguignon or, as it was written on the menu, "Boeuf à la Bourguignonne." The first mouthful brought me back through time; suddenly it was Thursday night. Yes, it was stew. And so is this.

The Staples: Make sure that these are all on hand: butter, bay leaf, thyme, salt, pepper, sugar, flour, garlic, olive oil.

The Shopping List: Top round beef (three pounds), one half pound bacon, small white onions (fifteen to twenty), mushrooms (one pound), potatoes (two pounds, new potatoes if available), tomato paste (small can), a can of beef bouillon, two bottles of red Burgundy wine, Grand Marnier liqueur (small bottle), parsley, celery, one carrot, a loaf of French or Italian bread, large eating oranges.

3 PM: First we brown the beef. Cut the beef into bite-sized cubes. Put half a cup of flour into a brown paper bag and shake the beef chunks until they are coated with flour.

In a heavy frying pan over medium-high heat, melt a half stick of butter and add a splash of olive oil. Brown the cubes of meat quickly, moving them around so that they cook briefly on all sides. Then transfer them to an ovenproof casserole. If the frying pan tends to dry out, add more butter and oil.

3:30 PM: Preheat the oven to 350 degrees. Using the same heavy frying pan over medium-low heat, melt some butter and add two small white onions, chopped very fine. Then add the carrot, peeled and chopped fine; a stalk of celery—including the leaves—rinsed clean, then chopped fine; and two cloves of garlic, minced. Cook these over medium-low heat until they are softened and then remove from the heat.

Add a tablespoon of tomato paste to the pan and stir in three tablespoons of flour. Again putting the pan over medium heat, stir constantly until the flour just starts to brown. Now add half a bottle of Burgundy and the beef bouillon. Continue to stir gently until the mixture comes to a boil. Lower the heat and stir until the sauce is thick and smooth, then pour it over the meat in the casserole dish.

And now the seasonings. Chop four or five sprigs of parsley fine and add these, along with a large bay leaf, a pinch of thyme, and a generous amount of salt and pepper. Pop the casserole into the oven. It should take between two and a half and three hours before the meat is sufficiently tender.

5:30 PM: Peel the new potatoes and cook in boiling water until a fork pierces them easily (approximately twenty minutes).

Fry the bacon, cut into small pieces. Peel away the outer layers of the remaining onions and brown them with the bacon. As they are cooking, add a splash of red wine. After they are slightly browned, add the onions and bacon to the casserole dish in the oven.

6 PM: Rinse the mushrooms and cut away the stem tips. Then, leaving the mushrooms whole, sauté them gently over a medium-low heat, again in butter. Keep warm along with the potatoes.

6:10 PM: Now for the garlic bread. Slice the loaf lengthwise either once or twice. Butter one side of each section and add slivers of garlic. Then place in the oven for ten to fifteen minutes, until the butter has melted and the bread has started to brown.

6:20 PM: Remove the garlic bread and carefully scrape away all the garlic slivers. (*Danger! All* of them.) Add the potatoes and mushrooms to the Beef Bourguignon and serve piping hot, accompanied by a bottle of red wine. Then bring out the garlic bread for the mopping-up operation. This will all be followed by thick slices of peeled oranges, lightly sugared and flavored with just a splash of Grand Marnier.

A final note. Whether you call this dish Beef Bourguignon or just plain stew, try to save some leftovers. If you've done your job properly, this may not be so easy. What you'll do with the leftovers is this: add some chopped onions, some other vegetables, some bouillon or water, some seasonings. What you will have then is a first-rate soup. Or *potage*. All I know is that we called it soup and we knew it was Friday.

MENU 29

Shrimp Scampi
Rice Pilaf
Baked Tomatoes Provençal
Grapefruit

The one true test of any cook is a diet. This year's hot new diet is called the Scarsdale Diet, and it is the truest test of them all. I'm not talking about the breakfast, which consists of unbuttered toast, unsugared coffee, and unsweetened grapefruit. I can think of only one sensible thing to do with a breakfast like that, and cooking isn't it.

The real challenge to the cook comes with the other two meals, the so-called lunch and the alleged dinner. One menu on the Scarsdale Diet, for example, recommends "cottage cheese, cabbage, and two eggs." I can't get this combination out of my mind. What do you do with cottage cheese, cabbage, and two eggs? A strange borscht? A sloppy salad? A disgusting omelet? What then? My feeling is that combinations like this one may well explain the diet's success. If that doesn't ruin your appetite, nothing ever will.

However, it shouldn't be necessary to go to those extremes. Here's a meal that may stretch any diet a little bit, but it shouldn't totally destroy it.

The Staples: Make sure that these are all on hand: salt, pepper, butter, basil, thyme, oregano, garlic, rosemary, savory.

The Shopping List: Two pounds of shrimp, whole wheat bread (one loaf), olive oil, one box brown rice, one can beef bouillon, one bunch parsley, five large tomatoes, one bunch scallions, one onion, chives, carrots, celery, lemon, three grapefruit, grated Parmesan cheese (four ounces).

Prepare in Advance: The seasoned bread crumbs.

It is, of course, possible to buy ready-made bread crumbs in the supermarket. But what you'll have here is high-nutrition bread crumbs.

The best starting point would be a loaf of whole wheat bread three or four days old. If the bread is still soft, dry it out in the oven. Spread the slices on a cookie sheet in a 250-degree oven and, when the bread is thoroughly dry, put it into the blender along with the grated Parmesan cheese and the following seasonings: a large pinch of chopped parsley, some chopped chives, a pinch of basil, another of rosemary, and one of savory. Blend together and store in a cool spot.

Also Prepare in Advance: The shrimps. Shell the shrimps and remove the veins. The shells will come off easily, and the veins can be removed with either a sharp paring knife or a toothpick. Then—and here's an old dieter's trick designed to fool the eye—slice the shrimps in half lengthwise.

Place the shrimp halves in a flat baking dish. Add two thirds cup of olive oil (sorry about that). Chop up three cloves of garlic and one third of the parsley and add that. Then add a large pinch of oregano, some salt and pepper, and one fourth cup of the seasoned bread crumbs.

Mix all this together and let it stand at room temperature

for a couple of hours, or in the refrigerator overnight.

5:15 PM: In a pot with a tight cover, melt half a stick of butter (oops, sorry again) over medium heat. Add a cup of dry brown rice and stir it until it browns slightly in the butter. Now add half an onion, chopped fine, and two and a half cups of liquid (the canned bouillon and water). While you are doing this, eat two raw carrots. Rice Pilaf is one of those experimental dishes that invite varied additions. Chopped mushrooms, diced peppers, chopped scallions, minced parsley, crushed tomatoes—anything goes.

5:45 PM: Since we're using brown rice instead of white rice, the cooking time will be about twice the normal amount. Cover the pot tightly and cook the rice for about forty-five minutes over a very low flame.

5:50 PM: And now, the Tomatoes Provençal. Preheat the oven to 350 degrees. Rinse and dry the tomatoes. Using a sharp knife, cut a circle out of the top of each tomato. Spoon the pulp of the tomato into a mixing bowl, and then turn the tomato shells over so that they'll drain while you're putting together the filling.

Chop up the rest of the parsley and add that to the tomato pulp, along with two cloves of garlic, minced fine, a pinch of thyme, the juice of half a lemon, three scallions, chopped fine, a generous amount of salt and pepper, and enough seasoned bread crumbs to bind the mixture. Fill the tomato shells with the stuffing.

6 PM: Grease a casserole dish lightly, put the stuffed tomatoes into it, and cover tightly. Place the covered dish in the preheated oven. Eat two stalks of celery.

6:30 PM: Increase the oven heat to 450 degrees. Put the shrimps into the hot oven and remove the cover from the tomato casserole. Eat another carrot.

6:40 PM: Remove the tomatoes from the oven and keep warm. Check the rice. Set the shrimps under a broiler for a final five minutes. Eat another stalk of celery.

6:45 PM: Serve dinner. Go lightly with the shrimps but try not to count calories. A few shrimps, a little rice, as much tomato as you want. And for dessert, a half grapefruit, no sugar. Why that? It's just to keep you honest.

MENU 30

Chicken Cacciatore
Buttered Spaghetti
Cucumbers in Dill Sauce
Sugared Grapes
Dry Red Wine

People who write cookbooks are always asked where they get their recipes. Often they will claim that they are family heirlooms handed down from one generation to the next, or that they are dramatic new versions of golden oldies. Only occasionally will it be claimed that the dish is a pure invention. This is one of those occasions. That's right. I am the man who invented Chicken Cacciatore.

A word of explanation may be in order here. I invented Chicken Cacciatore in much the way Helmut Matuso invented the typewriter. Helmut, you may remember, spent sixty years in the Swiss Alps living as a recluse. During those long years as a hermit, Helmut was inventing a machine to make printing appear on a page. You would hit a button—say, the "A" button—on a keyboard and the same letter—"A," in this instance—would appear on a page of paper.

Making the components of hand-carved wood and rubber bands, Helmut finally finished work on his *machine à écrire* ("machine to write"). He carried it down to the main patent office in Zurich. Unfortunately, the year was 1974, and, as he walked into the patent office, he heard the terrible clatter of electric typewriters. Helmut, incidentally, is back on his mountaintop, where he is working on a machine that plays music from revolving disks.

The full story of how I invented Chicken Cacciatore will follow. Here's how you can do it.

The Staples: Make sure that these are all on hand: salt, pepper, flour, confectioners' sugar, olive oil, vinegar, garlic, thyme, oregano, eggs.

The Shopping List: Two frying chickens (cut into serving pieces), two large onions, two green peppers, two cucumbers, one half pound fresh mushrooms, fresh dill, sweet white grapes (two pounds), one small can tomato paste, one large can Italian plum tomatoes, one pound spaghetti, butter, one small container of sour cream, grated Parmesan cheese (four ounces), one bottle dry red wine.

4:30 PM: Put half a cup of flour into a brown paper bag and add large pinches of salt and pepper. Shake the pieces of chicken in the bag.

Place a large, heavy frying pan over moderate heat. Put a chunk of butter and a splash of olive oil into the pan. When the butter has melted, add the chicken and cook until the pieces are browned on all sides.

Remove the chicken from the skillet. Add more oil and butter. Chop the onions and put them in the pan. Next, add the green peppers, also chopped, two cloves of garlic, minced, a large pinch of oregano, another of thyme, and salt and pepper. Stir.

When the chopped onions are tender, add a cup of red wine, the tomato paste, and the plum tomatoes.

5 PM: Add the chicken pieces to the pot and cover tightly. Cook over low heat, checking every now and then to make sure the chicken isn't sticking.

5:30 PM: Rinse the grapes and break the large bunches into small clumps. Beat together the whites of three eggs for just a couple of minutes, until they are thick but not stiff. Dip the grapes into the egg whites and dust them with powdered sugar. Keep cold until ready to serve.

5:55 PM: Rinse the mushrooms and cut away the tips of the stems. Add the mushrooms to the chicken for the final half hour of cooking.

6 PM: Start a large pot of water boiling. For a pound of spaghetti—or any pasta—use between four and six quarts of water. Add a small handful of salt and a tablespoon of oil to the water.

When the water comes to a full boil—that should be in twenty minutes or so—add the pasta slowly, a small bit at a time, trying not to interrupt the boil. (Danger! Never cover a pasta pot, or you'll spend the next ten minutes mopping up the stove.) Check for doneness in about eight minutes; the spaghetti should be chewy but never tough.

6:15 PM: The salad. Peel the cucumbers and slice them as thin as possible. Add a dressing made up of half a container of sour cream, a large pinch of minced dill, a small shot of vinegar, and a generous amount of salt and pepper.

6:30 PM: Check the chicken to make sure that it is cooked through. Serve it beside a generous helping of the spaghetti, to which you have added butter, salt, pepper, and the Parmesan cheese. Serve the cucumbers on the side.

As you first bite into the Chicken Cacciatore, you may well wonder how such a marvelous dish was invented. Let me tell you how it came about. (Incidentally, you may find this an even simpler way of cooking the dish.) One day I found myself with a large quantity of leftover spaghetti sauce. As an experiment, I stewed some chicken in that leftover spaghetti sauce. A guest that evening smacked her lips and said, "My, this is a wonderful Chicken Cacciatore." And that is what I decided to call my new invention.

MENU 31

Veal Français
Broccoli with Garlic
Baked Rice and Onions
Vin Rosé
Baked Apples Flambé

During their bachelorhood most men will learn to cook at least a few meals. This is the only sure way of staving off the number-one threat to all bachelors: outright starvation. Not to mention the other advantages. There are few sights more memorable than the way a young woman's eyes will soften in the light cast by flaming crepes suzette served by an earnest young man.

It used to be possible for bachelors to get by with just half a dozen truly impressive dinners. By the time they ran through their full repertory, one of two things would have happened: The young woman would have seen through him and moved along, or she would have done what women were always expected to do—she would have taken over the cooking.

But times do change. And now that you're expected to do your share of the cooking, you may want to revive one of those romantic meals from your bachelorhood. When women's magazines advise their readers on how to perk up a flagging marriage, they inevitably suggest a candlelit dinner for two. Well, now it's your turn.

So tonight you're going to get rid of the kids—send them off to Eddie's Pizza and the latest disco movie. Put the new candles into the old candlesticks. Get the wine on ice. Get yourself showered and shaved and lotioned, and when she comes in, weary after another long day at the office, you're going to be waiting there with a big kiss and she's going to say, "Hey, are you back on the sauce again?"

The Staples: Make sure that these are all on hand: salt, flour, sugar, olive oil, milk, rum, garlic, rice, and, oh, yes, candlesticks.

The Shopping List: Scallops of veal (one pound), vin rosé, two lemons, broccoli (one pound), three large onions, butter, baking apples, grated Parmesan cheese (four ounces), parsley, candles.

Shopping Note: Veal Français—veal with lemon—may be a meal that can soften a woman's heart; it is also a budget-buster that can flatten a wallet.

The most important part of preparing tonight's meal takes place in the market, not the kitchen. Look for veal that is white instead of pink—the paler the meat, the younger and more tender it is. Ask the butcher to flatten the slices of veal to a thickness of about a quarter of an inch. And when you get the meat home, soak it in a bowl of milk until you're ready to cook it.

4:50 PM: First, the baked rice. Preheat the oven to 325 degrees. Start a large pot of water boiling, exactly as if you were going to cook spaghetti. When it is boiling briskly, drop in half a cup of rice. After the water returns to a boil, cook the rice for just five minutes. Then, using a colander, drain away the water.

Place a heavy casserole dish over a medium flame and melt a stick of butter. Finely chop the onions and stir them into the melted butter. Now add the rice, a dash of salt, and half the Parmesan cheese.

5:30 PM: Cover the casserole dish and put it into the pre-heated oven. It should complete cooking in just one hour.

5:40 PM: Start the water boiling in a covered pot. Prepare the broccoli for cooking by cutting away the tough lower portion of the stalks. Cut the remaining stalks into half-inch chunks and boil these for about five minutes before adding the flowerets. Cook these for another five minutes and then drain away the water.

In a frying pan, heat up one fourth cup of olive oil and a clove of garlic, minced fine. When the oil is hot, add the broccoli and cook until it is just tender. Sprinkle on the rest of the Parmesan cheese, cover the pan, and turn the heat way down until the vegetable is served.

6 PM: Remove the veal slices from the milk and dust them with flour. Place a large skillet over medium-high heat with half a stick of butter and a splash of olive oil. When the butter has melted, brown the veal quickly on both sides, frying it for four or five minutes on a side. Then add the juice of one lemon and a shot of your dinner wine. Lower the heat, cut a second lemon into thin slices, and spread them over the veal. Sprinkle with chopped parsley and cover the pan over the lowest possible heat until ready to serve.

6:15 PM: The baked apples. Peel the apples and cut out the cores. (If you look in the drawer over there, you just may find an apple corer. No? Lotsa luck, then.) Put the cored apples into a baking dish with half an inch of water. Place two tablespoons of sugar into the center of each apple and top it with a chunk of butter.

6:30 PM: As you remove the baked rice from the oven, put in the apples and increase the heat to 350 degrees. They should be baked just as you are finishing the rest of the dinner, in about half an hour. By this time you should be discovering the shortest distance to a woman's heart.

Heat some rum in a small saucepan and spoon it over the apples. Just before serving, touch the apples with a match. As the rum goes up in flames, your wife should completely melt. If not, it's time for you to ask yourself a serious question: Can this marriage be saved?

MENU 32

Whole Wheat Bread
French Onion Soup
Delmonico Salad
Cinnamon Buns

Back to basics. I know of no cooking experience so basic, or quite so satisfying, as the baking of bread—maybe because it deeply involves each of the five senses.

The sense of touch, for example. The cook is up to his elbows in bread dough, as closely involved with his work as a sculptor. Smell: No perfume from the blossoms of Araby can match the simple aroma of baking bread. Sight: Name any vision more enticing than the picture of butter melting on hot-from-the-oven bread. Taste, to be sure. And where, you ask, does the sense of sound come in? Well, if you don't hear cheers tonight, you never will.

This recipe came from my grandmother, Libby Robinson, and it has been handed down through the generations the way more affluent—but not richer—families might pass along brooches.

The Staples: Make sure that these are all on hand: salt, pepper, brown sugar (or honey), eggs, butter, olive oil, wine vinegar, flour, Tabasco sauce, cinnamon. Also: bread pans, a wooden spoon, a large mixing bowl, a rolling pin.

The Shopping List: One pound of bacon, whole wheat flour (five pounds), yeast (three cakes or envelopes), five large Bermuda onions, two cans consommé, grated cheeses (Gruyère and Parmesan), Roquefort cheese (four ounces), one box raisins, head of lettuce.

Prepare in Advance: The bread. (Allow a whole afternoon for the baking.)

Begin with the bacon, frying it in a large skillet over medium heat. Allow the cooked bacon to drain on paper towels and set aside the bacon fat.

Put one cup of warm water—it should feel pleasantly warm to your wrist—into a small bowl and add a heaping teaspoon of brown sugar (or honey) and the yeast.

Begin the batter in a large mixing bowl, We'll start with half a cup of bacon fat. Purists may shudder at this, and I must admit I've never seen another bread recipe that called for bacon fat. However, I've never tasted a bread this good, Perhaps there's a connection.

To the bacon fat, my grandmother would add two cups of raw or brown sugar (but honey is an acceptable substitute), a tablespoon of salt, then one quart of very warm water.

And now the flour. Add the whole wheat flour one cup at a time, beating each cupful into the batter with a wooden spoon. It would be nice to give accurate flour measurements, but my grandmother never bothered too much with measuring. You'll probably use twelve or thirteen cups in all. But now keep adding until the dough stiffens (about nine cups).

In a small mixing bowl, beat two eggs for just a couple of seconds and add them to the batter. And now add the original yeast mixture. You'll need more flour—white flour this time. Add just enough so the dough becomes a large ball that you can remove to a bread board (about three cups).

(*Caution!* Be sure to dust your working surface with plenty of flour.)

Now the kneading. Allow at least fifteen minutes for kneading the bread. Do not tear the dough but fold it over onto itself, using the heels of your hands to apply most of the pressure. Add more flour as long as the dough adheres to the table or board. When the dough can be handled without the addition of more flour, it's close to ready.

Carefully oil the inside of your largest mixing bowl and put the ball of dough inside this. Cover it with a dampened dish towel and set it in a warm spot, perhaps near a radiator. The dough should rise to double its size in about an hour. Punch the dough back down to its original size and let it rise again (about fifty minutes).

When it has doubled its size, slice the dough into four equal parts. Oil the inside of the bread pans. Roll the dough balls into log shapes and press three of them into the bread pans.

Now for the cinnamon rolls. Using a rolling pin, roll the fourth dough ball into a thin sheet. Sprinkle brown sugar and cinnamon lightly over the entire surface. Then dot it with little pieces of butter and raisins. Roll this into a log and, using a sharp knife, cut off inch-wide slices. Place the slices on a greased cookie sheet.

As the dough rises a third time (about thirty to forty minutes), preheat the oven to 350 degrees. Bake the bread for fifty minutes, then test—if the bread is done, it will make a hollow thumping sound when you rap against it. The cinnamon buns will be done in less time (about thirty minutes).

Also Prepare in Advance: The soup. Peel the onions and slice them thin. Melt half a stick of butter in a large pan over medium heat and add the onion rings. Cook them until they become transparent, then add two teaspoons of white flour. Cook for a couple of minutes, stirring, and then add the consommé and two cans of water.

Add salt and pepper to taste and simmer for at least thirty minutes. Just before serving, top with the grated cheeses.

Finally, the Salad: Rinse, dry, and break up a head of lettuce. Add the bacon, broken into pieces, and the Delmonico dressing—half a cup of olive oil, three tablespoons of wine vinegar, the crumbled Roquefort cheese, salt, pepper, and a shot of Tabasco sauce.

MENU 33

New England Pot Roast
Potato Pancakes
Broiled Pineapple

Time is money . . . time is money . . . time *is* money. This great truth has been hammered into us ever since we first got paid by the hour. The great truth is most easily remembered on weekends, especially when man is asked to get out the storm windows or cook the dinner. However, on weekends it can also be forgotten, especially when man is asked to spend long hours chasing a tiny white ball around a golf course or whole days parked in front of the tube watching gridiron godzillas bump noggins.

Today's meal is a case in point. To put together a proper pot roast takes the better part of an afternoon—more than likely an afternoon already allocated to watching events set in distant exotic cities: South Bend, Dallas, or Green Bay.

Today, the old two-birds-with-one-stone trick. Actually, there is no big trick to preparing this meal at the same time you're watching a football game. In fact, you'll find it a not unpleasant and intensely American combination—the spicy and heartwarming aroma of a pot roast bubbling gently on the stove top, the televised sight of bone-crunching violence on the gridiron.

The Staples: Make sure that these are all on hand: salt, pepper, flour, cinnamon, cloves, cooking oil, bay leaf, rum, eggs, and butter.

The Shopping List: One pot roast (preferably bottom round, between one and five pounds), consommé (one can), small white onions (two pounds), carrots (one pound), potatoes (three pounds), one large Bermuda onion, one four-ounce jar horseradish sauce, one fresh pineapple, one small jar applesauce, one bottle red wine.

But when do you manage to do the cooking? Why, during the natural breaks in the action, of course. During the pregame show, the time-outs, the halftime festivities, the slow-motion replays of the other team's touchdowns, and whenever Howard Cosell delivers an opinion.

Prepare Before the Opening Kickoff: The meat.

Sprinkle salt and freshly ground pepper over the entire surface of the meat and rub it in with the heel of a spoon. Now do the same thing with several tablespoons of flour.

Put four tablespoons of oil into a heavy casserole placed on medium-high heat. When the oil is hot, add the meat. Brown the meat on all sides, tending it closely to make sure that it doesn't burn.

When the meat has been browned, add the can of consommé and an equal amount of red wine. Then add a teaspoon of cinnamon, five whole cloves, and a bay leaf.

This next step will appeal to anyone who is fond of torturing his wife. (And if you aren't fond of torturing your wife, what are you doing sitting on your duff, watching a football game on a beautiful day like this?) First, make sure she is watching you. Then calmly dump an entire jar of horseradish sauce (*Danger!* The four-ounce size!) into the pot. All of it. All at once. If your wife can watch you do this without screaming, the marriage is a sound one.

What happens, of course, is that the slow simmering robs the horseradish of its bite. Allow the mixture to come to a boil, then put the heat on low and cover the pot tightly.

During the First-Quarter Break: Prepare the vegetables.

Peel the small white onions and set them aside. Peel the carrots, cut them into thirds, and set them aside. Turn the pot roast over.

During the Halftime Ceremonies: Add the carrots and the onions to the pot.

During Interview with Recently Fired Coach: Start the potato pancakes going. Peel the large Bermuda onion and grate it. Peel the potatoes and grate them and add them to the onion. Beat two eggs lightly, stir them in, and add two tablespoons of flour. Now, back to the game.

During Close-ups of the Dallas Cowgirls: Do nothing, Some things require full concentration.

During the Final Time-Outs: Set a large, heavy frying pan over medium heat. Add a chunk of butter and a splash of cooking oil.

At Game's End: The final preparations.

Add large spoonfuls of the potato mixture to the frying pan, cook the pancakes until they are golden brown on one side, then flip over. When they are cooked on both sides, drain on paper towels while a new batch is being cooked.

Meanwhile, test the pot roast to make sure it is done. The total cooking time should be around three hours. When it is done, the meat is easily pierced by a fork.

Next prepare the dessert. Cut the pineapple into thick slices and then cut away the skin and the eyes. Put the pineapple slices under the broiler for a short time until they are softened, then add a small splash of rum.

The Proper Time to Serve Dinner: Between games.

Cut the beef into very thin slices and serve with vegetables and sauce. Serve the potato pancakes with a spoonful of applesauce (or sour cream). Follow with the warm pineapple. And now you can switch channels.

MENU 34

Bloody Marys
Eggs Benedict
Apple Crisps
Hot Coffee

The Sunday morning brunch. Nothing seems so modern, so contemporary, so with-it as this new American institution. Although the word itself—a melding of *breakfast* and *lunch*—is new, the concept is not.

Diamond Jim Brady, for example, was a well-known brunch-goer. Rising at a later hour than the laboring men of his era, Diamond Jim made it a practice to arrive at his favorite restaurant at 10:30 AM, well into the slack period separating breakfast and lunch.

No sooner was the famed bon vivant seated than the first course would arrive: fresh juice followed by hot muffins, eggs, and hominy grits. As he began to chow down, the chef would set the pork chops and hotcakes on the griddle. And this, in turn, would be followed by a medium-rare steak and a side order of home fries. It was then Diamond Jim's habit to order three dozen oysters. Quite frequently this would carry him all the way to lunch.

While today's brunch is not quite that elaborate, it will suffice. In fact, it will make either a first-rate midmorning feast or a very pleasant dinner.

The Staples: Make sure that these are all on hand: salt, pepper, flour, sugar, cinnamon, coffee and cream, celery salt, horseradish, Tabasco sauce, Worcestershire sauce, vodka, white distilled vinegar.

The Shopping List: Tomato juice (large can), three large lemons, a dozen eggs, English muffins (one per person), ham slices (enough to cover English muffins), butter (half a pound), green cooking apples (half a dozen).

First, a word of warning. This one is not so simple as it may at first seem. As you get down to the wire, you're going to need some of the skills of a juggler and some of the skills of an efficiency expert.

10 AM: We begin with the Apple Crisps. Preheat the oven to 350 degrees. Core and thinly slice the apples and arrange them in a greased jelly roll pan. (*Warning!* It is absolutely necessary to grease the pan.)

In a separate bowl put a stick of butter, a cup of sugar, and half a cup of flour. Using two knives, cut the butter into the flour and mix it up until it is of a crumblike consistency. Place the mixture over the apple slices and sprinkle with cinnamon. Place in the oven for forty-five minutes.

10:30 AM: And now's as good a time as any to put together the Bloody Marys. To each cup of tomato juice, add three jiggers of vodka, a teaspoon of lemon juice, a healthy dash of Worcestershire sauce, a few drops of Tabasco sauce, a scattering of salt, pepper, and celery salt. And—the most important ingredient of all—a heaping teaspoon of horseradish sauce. This can be kept on ice until the rest of the meal is ready.

10:45 AM: Check the Apple Crisps in the oven and set the coffee to perking.

And now, the main event. You'll want to allow at least half an hour to make Eggs Benedict, and it may be helpful if you know what you're supposed to have when the time is up—toasted English muffins topped by slices of ham, topped by poached eggs, topped by hollandaise sauce.

We begin with the hollandaise sauce. You'll need a double boiler, another pot, a frying pan, and a wire whisk.

Put an inch of water into a frying pan and get it boiling. This will be used later for poaching the eggs, but now you'll need some of the boiling water.

In a second pot, over low heat, melt a stick of butter, making sure that it doesn't start to bubble or turn brown.

Heat water in the bottom part of the double boiler until it reaches the boiling point, then turn it down to low. Separate three egg yolks from the whites and put the yolks in the upper part of the double boiler. Beat the egg yolks with a wire whisk until they start to thicken and then add a full tablespoon of the boiling water from the frying pan. Beat again until it starts to thicken and add another tablespoon of boiling water, and a third, and finally a fourth.

Now turn the heat off completely. Remove the sauce from the stove. Add two tablespoons of lemon juice. Then, while still beating the sauce with the whisk, add the melted butter in a steady, slow stream. It should turn into a sauce with the consistency of mayonnaise, and then you'll add a dash of salt.

Should the sauce start to curdle at any time, add another tablespoon of boiling water and stir rapidly.

Set the sauce aside now while you assemble the rest of the ingredients, beginning with the poached eggs. To the water boiling in the frying pan add a teaspoon of white distilled vinegar. Break each egg very gently (*Danger! Very gently!*) into a small saucer and slide the egg carefully into the boiling water. As the eggs start to firm up in the boiling water, lower the heat and let simmer four or five minutes.

While the eggs are poaching, toast the English muffins and butter them, and heat the ham slices. Lay the ham on top of the muffins and then carefully remove the eggs from the water with a slotted spoon. Place the eggs on the ham slices and top with a generous portion of hollandaise sauce. Set them under the broiler for just a minute; then bring to the table piping hot, with the iced Bloody Marys and the hot coffee, followed by the Apple Crisps.

MENU 35

Rice-and-Cheese Casserole or
Potato-and-Pea Curry
Green Bean Salad
Fresh Fruit

Tonight, the blue plate special. No, *two* blue plate specials. A choice of meals designed for those rough times when you find yourself missing that one ingredient so important to all recipes—cold cash.

Well, in the first place, try not to let it get to you. There are some substitutes for that missing ingredient. Skill. Imagination. And maybe just a *soupçon* of courage.

In fact, there are some who would say that poverty was the best thing that ever happened to cooking. There's no trick to putting together a satisfactory little meal when you're starting out with half a dozen lobsters or a rack of lamb. However, when you find yourself staring at a bag of beans, a box of rice, and last month's unpaid bills—that's when you've got to be a cook.

The careful reader will observe that there is no meat on tonight's menu. That is hardly accidental. Anyone forced to cook on a budget soon learns the virtues of vegetarianism. However, don't apologize. Whichever main dish you choose to make tonight—and the chances are that no one in the family has ever tasted either one—is a guaranteed show stopper. The rice-and-cheese casserole is a south-of-the-border sensation, and the all-vegetable curry is the most popular dish in India; give either one a try and you'll understand why.

The Staples: For cooking *both* dinners, make sure that these are all on hand: butter, milk, olive oil, wine vinegar, salt, pepper, cayenne pepper, cumin, dry mustard, turmeric, coriander, garlic.

The Shopping List: Again, for cooking *both* dinners: potatoes (three pounds), frozen peas (one box), brown rice, black-eyed peas, green chili peppers (small jar), ricotta cheese (one small container), cheddar cheese (one pound), fresh string beans (two pounds), two large onions, lettuce, yogurt (one small container), fresh fruit.

BLUE PLATE SPECIAL NO. 1:
RICE-AND-CHEESE CASSEROLE

5 PM: Cook two cups of dry brown rice according to the directions on the package. This will take about forty-five minutes. While the rice is cooking, cook one cup of black-eyed peas in water over medium-low heat until they are tender.

Remove both the rice and the black-eyed peas from the heat when done. Then, in a large skillet over medium heat, melt a chunk of butter and add a large onion that has been peeled and chopped fine and a cup of the green chili peppers, which have been cut into small pieces.

When the onions are cooked through, remove the pan from the heat and set aside. Now mix in the rice and the black-eyed peas.

In a separate mixing bowl place the ricotta cheese and add a splash of milk. Grate the cheddar cheese and add that. Stir together.

Butter the sides of a large casserole dish and add about a third of the rice mixture, an equal proportion of the cheese mixture, another layer of rice, and another layer of cheese. And then bake the casserole for forty minutes in a 350-degree oven.

BLUE PLATE SPECIAL NO. 2:
POTATO-AND-PEA CURRY

5:15 PM: Peel the potatoes and cut them into half-inch cubes.

Using a large skillet, heat half a stick of butter over medium-low heat. As the butter melts, add one teaspoon each of the following spices: cumin, salt, turmeric, coriander, and dry mustard. Then add half a teaspoon of cayenne pepper, unless you like your food very hot; then you'll add a little more.

Using a wooden spoon, stir the spices together and allow them to cook gently for a few minutes. Then add the potatoes. Continue to stir while the cubed potatoes are being browned and seasoned on all sides. Cook them for about ten minutes over medium heat.

When the potatoes are browned, add two cups of water. The potatoes will simmer for about twenty minutes; then you add the frozen peas. In about ten minutes more, when the peas are cocked, add the yogurt and mix well. The dish will be ready in five minutes.

Other vegetables can be added at will; I find both chopped peppers and diced carrots welcome additions. The resulting curry is so pungent and flavorful that—despite its potato content—it can be served over rice.

Prepare Anytime: The green bean salad. Cut away the tips of the fresh string beans and cook the beans in boiling water until they are just tender. Drain the beans, cool them, and slice them lengthwise.

Slice a large onion into very thin slices and mix them with the cooked beans. Add salt, pepper, half a cup of olive oil, the same amount of wine vinegar, and a fourth of a cup of water, plus three cloves of garlic, minced.

Mix this all together and store in the refrigerator. Just before serving, put the beans on a few leaves of lettuce and serve.

MENU 36

Roast Ducklings
Peas with Mushrooms
Wild Rice Casserole
Red Wine
Coffee
Brownies

A cook's life is made up of small milestones. The first hollandaise sauce that doesn't curdle. The first flaming dish without too much sizzle or fizzle. And tonight a monumental milestone: the first company dinner.

Oh, most of the meals we've put together here can be served—without fear or apology—to guests. But tonight's meal is not quite so simple as the others. Which is why you may want to test it first on the family. After all, even the most lavish Broadway show will have its out-of-town tryout. So see if it plays in the sticks and then send out invitations for, oh, six. And since tonight is a company dinner, let's set the time a little later than usual, say 7:30.

The Staples: Make sure that these are all on hand; salt, pepper, Tabasco sauce, Dijon mustard, curry powder, garlic, wheat germ, butter, coffee (and accompanying cream and sugar).

The Shopping List: Two ducks (under five pounds each), two boxes frozen peas, one and one half pounds of mushrooms, canned chicken broth (three cups), wild rice (one cup), sweetened condensed milk, graham cracker crumbs (one cup), raisins, chocolate chips (one small package), celery, one small onion, two lemons, one orange, one small jar honey, red wine.

The starting point for this recipe was a talk I once had with a Milwaukee food editor. She told me that the most popular recipe she ever wrote was a simple roast chicken basted with a combination of honey, lemon, mustard, and curry powder. If you try it, you'll understand why. And a nice bonus: It works as well with ducks. Perhaps the most common way of preparing duck is à l'orange—with an orange sauce. This is equally impressive and quite a bit less work.

Prepare in Advance: The brownies.

Preheat the oven to 325 degrees. Mix together the can of condensed milk, a cup of graham cracker crumbs, and a quarter cup of wheat germ. Stir in a large handful of raisins and the chocolate chips. Butter the inside of a rectangular 9-by-13-inch baking dish and pour in the batter. Bake for exactly thirty minutes, remove from the heat, and cut into small squares. Set aside.

Also to Be Prepared in Advance: The ducklings. If frozen, they should be thawed.

And the duck basting sauce. Mix together in a small bowl half a cup of honey, three garlic cloves, minced, a couple of shots of Tabasco sauce, a tablespoon of Dijon mustard, the juice of the lemons and the orange, and two to three tablespoons of curry powder.

Set aside.

And the vegetables. Rinse the mushrooms and cut off the tops of the stems. Slice them thin. Allow the green peas to thaw.

And the other vegetables that go with the wild rice. Cut five celery stalks into tiny pieces. Chop up the onion. Set these aside.

5:30 PM: Preheat the oven to 360 degrees.

First, the wild rice casserole. Rinse the wild rice in cool water before beginning. (*Caution!* Don't allow any of it to slip away; you won't, if you remember what you paid for it.) Take a casserole pan and butter the inside surface. Add two and a half cups of chicken broth, and the wild rice. Now the celery and the onion, and if you feel like it you can swipe a small handful of the sliced mushrooms. Put the cover on the casserole and pop it into the oven.

5:45 PM: Prepare the ducks. Take the curry-honey-lemon-orange mixture and smear it generously over—and inside—the birds. When you're placing them in the roasting pan, put them onto a metal rack, above the reach of the melted fat.

6 PM: Place the ducks in the oven with the wild rice casserole. Most of your work is done by this time. Greet the company. Smile. Have a drink. Oh, c'mon, relax a little. And every twenty minutes or so get up and baste the ducks with fresh coats of the honey mixture. Every now and then pierce the skin with a fork to let more fat escape. You may want to pour away the fat if there's too great an accumulation.

7 PM: Remove the rice casserole from the oven and keep it warm until ready to serve. If it shows signs of being too dry, add some of the remaining chicken broth. Now's a good moment to open the bottle of red wine and let it "breathe" for a while.

7:20 PM: Raise the oven temperature to 450 degrees to put a nice crisp finish on the ducks. Continue to baste.

And, in a skillet over medium heat, melt half a stick of butter. Add the sliced mushrooms and, in a couple of minutes, the peas. Then add a little salt and pepper and cook it until the vegetables are just tender. Lower the heat.

7:30 PM: Cut into one of the ducks to make sure that it is cooked to your liking. Check the rice. Plug in the coffee maker.

Your last challenge will be to carve the ducks. You'll need a sharp knife and a steady hand. Simply cut the ducks into quarters, then serve beside the wild rice, and the peas, and the wine, followed in due time by the coffee, and the brownies, and a profound sense of relief.

MENU 37

Coq au Vin
Hot French Bread
Beaujolais Wine
Chocolate Custard

We live in the golden age of specialized cooking tools. There is a special appliance this year for just cooking frankfurters, another for hamburger patties, a third for grilled cheese sandwiches. Doubtless someone somewhere is even now ironing the kinks out of a brand-new, personal, single-egg boiler. One of the most popular of the relatively new cooking appliances is called the crock pot, and there are at least a dozen models for the crock-potter to choose from.

What sells the crock pot is convenience. This is the scenario: The family cook wakes up early, tosses some meat and vegetables into a crock pot, flicks a switch, goes off to work, comes home in the evening, lifts the lid, and discovers—aha!—a ready-to-eat dinner still hot in the pot. Okay, that's the theory. Here's what happens in real life: Up in the AM... the meat and vegs... the switch... the job... back home... lift up the lid and—aha!—soup.

Instead of using this newfangled contraption, tonight we're going to use an old-fashioned pot on top of an old-fashioned range, and you're going to be cooking one of the great French classics, Coq au Vin.

The Staples: Make sure that these are all on hand: salt, pepper, butter, milk, eggs, bay leaves, garlic, thyme, parsley, vanilla.

The Shopping List; Roasting chicken (four to five pounds, cut into sections), bacon (four strips), Beaujolais wine (two bottles), small white onions (two pounds), two large onions, one half pound of mushrooms, parsley, sweet chocolate (six ounces), cream (one cup), French or Italian bread.

Prepare in Advance: The Chocolate Custard. Mix together one cup of milk and the cream and cook over medium heat. Stir in the sweet chocolate. When the chocolate has melted and just before the mixture comes to a boil, remove from the heat.

In a separate bowl, beat together six egg yolks and one teaspoon of vanilla. Add this to the chocolate mixture a little at a time, beating between additions. Refrigerate in the bowl.

4:45 PM: And now for the main course. You'll be using a heavy cast-iron pot with a tight-fitting lid. In the beginning—but only in the beginning—you'll put this over medium-high heat. Fry the bacon until it's cooked through, then remove the strips of bacon from the pot.

Rinse the chicken pieces under cool water. Salt and pepper them generously, then fry them in the bacon fat until they are lightly browned on all sides. If more fat is needed, add a chunk of butter. Remove the chicken pieces from the pot.

5:10 PM: Peel and chop the onions and sauté them in the same pot, adding butter as necessary. Cook them until tender. Add about three fourths of a bottle of Beaujolais and turn the heat to high, allowing the wine to cook down for a few minutes. (*Caution!* Don't try to "cheap out" with inferior wine; the difference between Coq au Vin and chicken stew is the quality of the wine.)

As the wine is cooking, add two bay leaves, three cloves of garlic, minced fine, a pinch of thyme, a small handful of parsley, chopped, and the bacon slices, crumbled.

And, finally, the chicken pieces. The wine should just cover the chicken. If more is needed, add it. Then turn the heat to low and cover the pot tightly.

6 PM: Peel the small white onions and cut the tops from the mushroom stems—but do not slice either vegetable.

In a small frying pan over medium heat, melt a large chunk of butter. Add the peeled onions and sauté them, shaking the pan from time to time so that they are lightly browned on all sides. The total cooking time should be about ten minutes.

Set the onions to one side and, using the same pan, sauté the whole mushrooms in butter.

6:15 PM: Add the onions and the mushrooms to the pot. Open the second bottle of Beaujolais.

6:20 PM: Preheat the oven to 350 degrees. Slice the loaf of French bread lengthwise. Butter both sides and add minced garlic or a combination of minced garlic and minced parsley. Bake until the butter has melted and the bread has started to brown. The bread will be used in your mopping-up action.

6:30 PM: Remove the pot from the fire. If the sauce seems too watery, remove the other ingredients for a moment and boil it down some more. If it seems too thick, try it that way—it'll be delicious.

MENU 38

Garlic Bread
Tossed Greens
Cabbage Borscht or
Clam Chowder or
Split-Pea Soup
Mixed Cheeses

It is possible that Thomas Fuller overstated the case for soup when, nearly 400 years ago, he wrote, "Of soup and love, the first is best."

Fuller could not have been thinking of soups that serve as preamble to a meal—those pale consommés and wan bouillons, those see-through soups that are chilled or jellied or ganished with chives. No, what he had in mind was a soup that surrenders itself as readily to fork as spoon, a soup that doesn't come before a meal but is, indeed, a meal.

Love or soup? Fortunately, this is not a choice many of us feel compelled to make. However, on a cold winter night, with snow coming down on the slant and with the wind snapping at the windows, the question might not be decided too easily. Tonight it's soup.

CABBAGE BORSCHT

Ingredients: Beef (boneless chuck, two to three pounds), beef marrow bones (two pounds, cracked) a large turnip, two onions, three carrots, cabbage (one small head), celery, parsley, garlic, canned tomatoes (one large can), sauerkraut (one pound), sour cream, salt, pepper, bay leaf, fresh dill.

Time Required: Four hours. Preheat the oven to 450 degrees. Peel and dice the onions, carrots, and turnip. Slice the celery stalks and leaves. Place all this in a roasting pan with the meat and the bones and put them into the oven for twenty-five minutes.

Remove the pan from the oven and scrape the contents— including a few tablespoons of the melted fat—into a large soup kettle. Add eight cups of water and bring to a boil over high heat, then lower the heat to medium-low. As froth forms on the surface of the soup, remove it with a ladle.

Now add a large can of tomatoes, a small handful of parsley, another of fresh dill, a bay leaf, two cloves of garlic, minced, and some salt and pepper. Cover the pot and cook over low heat for two hours.

Add the cabbage, shredded, and the sauerkraut. Cook for another hour. The meat should be tender, falling-apart tender. Serve each bowl of soup with a dollop of sour cream and a pinch of dill.

CLAM CHOWDER

Ingredients: Bacon (five strips), fifty fresh chowder clams, two onions, one green pepper, celery, potatoes (two pounds), milk, light cream, salt, pepper.

Time Required: An hour and a half. Scrub and rinse the clams. Place them in a covered pot with six cups of cold water over high heat. When the water comes to a boil, reduce the heat and simmer until the clam shells open.

Cut the bacon into small pieces and cook in a large frying pan over medium heat. Peel and chop the onions and add them to the frying bacon. Chop up a green pepper and a stalk of celery, leaves included, and add.

When the clam shells have all opened, remove the meat from the shells and chop it. Add the clam meat to the frying pan. Before adding the rest of the clam broth, strain the sand away with a piece of cheesecloth.

Peel the potatoes, dice them, and add them to the mixture. In twenty minutes or so, when the potatoes are tender, add two cups of milk and one cup of light cream, as well as a generous amount of salt and pepper.

SPLIT-PEA SOUP

Ingredients: One ham bone (this is an ideal soup to make the day after you've had baked ham), split peas (two cups, dried), onion, celery, carrots, garlic, bay leaf, thyme, salt, pepper, cayenne pepper, croutons.

Time Required: Three hours. This same basic recipe—starting with a ham bone and as much of the ham as you've been able to salvage—works well with almost any dried bean, especially with lentils, kidney beans, black beans, and white pea beans. Whatever you settle on, rinse them carefully and soak them overnight.

Put the ham bone into a soup kettle with between two and three quarts of water. Add a large onion, peeled and chopped, three or four stalks of celery, chopped, including some of the leaves, two carrots, peeled and chopped, two cloves of garlic, minced, a bay leaf, a pinch of thyme and another of cayenne pepper, and salt and pepper.

Bring the water to a boil rapidly and then lower the heat. Simmer until the split peas are tender. Some would recommend that you remove the bone and run the rest of the soup through a blender; my feeling is that it should be left as is, served with some of the ham in each bowl and topped with a handful of croutons.

Once you've made the soup of your choice, the rest of the meal is a snap. Garlic bread—just slice a loaf of French or Italian bread down the middle, butter it, dot it with minced garlic, and bake for ten or fifteen minutes at 300 degrees. Then scrape off the garlic bits. The salad will be whatever greens are available, tossed with oil (three parts) and vinegar (one part). Beer and crackers would go very well with the clam chowder; try a hearty red wine with the other soups.

MENU 39

Broiled Lamb with Lemon-and-Caper Sauce
Spaetzle
Watercress Salad
Raspberry Ice
Red Wine

The reason we have not had many lamb recipes is the same reason we have not had many caviar recipes: because the kind of investment one makes in a matched set of loin chops is enough to take away your appetite.

It is not, however, because cooking lamb presents any problems. On the contrary. With most cuts of lamb, you don't have to do much more than put them fairly near an ongoing fire.

But of course, that would not be complicated enough to satisfy most cooks. They would be happier with the recipe described by Porthos, one of the original Three Musketeers. Porthos began with the whole lamb. He then watched as his cook "boned the lamb as he would bone a fowl, leaving the skin on, however, which formed a brown crust all over the animal." The boned lamb was stuffed, filled with sausages and larks, and then baked, with these somewhat picturesque results: "When it is cut in beautiful slices, in the same way that one would cut an enormous sausage, a rose-colored gravy issues forth, which is as agreeable to the eye as it is exquisite to the palate."

Well, times change. And so do tastes. So perhaps this time out we'll try it a simpler way.

The Staples: Make sure that these are all on hand: salt, pepper, cayenne pepper, eggs, olive oil, wine vinegar, garlic, arrowroot, butter, red wine, Grand Marnier.

The Shopping List: One leg of lamb (six pounds or more, boned by your butcher), one lemon, capers (one small bottle), three medium-sized onions, one red Italian onion, watercress (two bunches), chicken broth (one can), spaetzle (one box, available in food specialty stores), frozen raspberries (two boxes), cream.

Prepare the Day Before: The marinade for the lamb. In a shallow broiling pan, mix together these ingredients: three cloves of garlic, minced, one half cup of olive oil, the juice of half a lemon, one half cup of red wine, freshly ground black pepper, and salt. Peel the onions, slice them thin, and mix them into the marinade.

Place the boned leg of lamb in the marinade and turn it over a couple of times. Refrigerate until the next day. Every now and then turn the piece of meat over. Remove it from the refrigerator a couple of hours before cooking it.

5 PM: We'll begin with the watercress salad. Rinse the watercress and pat it dry. Cut the hard stems away. Cut the red onion into thin slices and add these rings to the salad. The dressing can be made now, then added at the last minute: three parts olive oil, one part wine vinegar, salt and pepper, and one clove of garlic, minced fine.

5:15 PM: The Raspberry Ice. Mix the two packages of raspberries with one third cup of Grand Marnier and run through the blender or food processor until smooth. Return to the freezer, to be served later in dessert cups with several spoons of fresh cream.

5:30 PM: The Lemon-and-Caper Sauce for the lamb. This is the only tricky part to tonight's meal. It's tricky because you'll be using a double boiler and egg yolks. One misstep equals scrambled eggs.

While the water is heating in the bottom half of the double boiler, stir together three egg yolks in the upper portion. Add the juice of half a lemon, a teaspoon of arrowroot, a dash of salt, and a couple of shakes of cayenne pepper. Keep stirring as the water heats up. Add a cup of the chicken broth and continue stirring until the sauce starts to thicken. Remove the double boiler from the heat and continue stirring for a couple of minutes. Keep the sauce warm over the-hot water until ready to serve. Just before serving add a small handful of capers.

5:45 PM: Start a pot of water boiling for the spaetzle. Following the directions on the box, cook the spaetzle just as you would cook pasta. The tiny dumplings should be cooked in furiously boiling water, drained at the proper moment, and served with butter, salt, and pepper.

6 PM: And now for the leg of lamb. Preheat the broiler so it will be at its hottest when you put in the lamb. Drain the marinade away from the lamb. You will see that the boned leg of lamb is not of an even thickness—it is "butterflied," and this uneven effect makes for interesting contrasts. The thickest portions of the meat should be cooked brown on the outside and pink on the inside; the thinner portions will be just right for those who like their meat well done.

Place the lamb on the rack and broil five inches from the heat for fifteen minutes. Allow another ten minutes on the second side and then test it for doneness. You'll slice the lamb in thin strips, the way you would slice a London broil, and serve it accompanied by the Lemon-and-Caper Sauce.

MENU 40

Quiche Lorraine
Amy's Famous Carrot Salad
Broiled Tomatoes Oregano
Applesauce

In the past, whenever we've made a pie here, we've taken the easy way out and used a frozen crust. This drives purists up the wall. Apparently, I couldn't have committed a greater *faux pas* if I had doused the main course with ketchup.

Numerous correspondents have assured me that *anyone* can make a piecrust. Some have sent in their own recipes, recipes usually bearing such names as "never-fail piecrust." Well, I have tried these offerings, and I am frankly wondering whether making a proper piecrust is a sex-linked trait, one of those things that women just naturally do better than men.

So this time out, no guarantees. This pie recipe, the best one I know, might be called "Mike's Sometimes-Fail Piecrust." We'll be using it for a quiche, and if I were you, I'd have some of those frozen crusts stashed in the freezer—just in case.

The Staples: Make sure that these are all on hand: salt, pepper, sugar, pastry flour, cider vinegar, peanut oil, olive oil, mustard, garlic salt, oregano, Worcestershire sauce, cinnamon.

The Shopping List: Bacon (one half pound), eggs, cheese (Swiss or Gruyère, one half pound), frozen piecrusts (just in case), lard, butter, light cream (two cups), carrots (two pounds), two medium-sized onions, green pepper, one small can tomato soup, tomatoes (five or six), six baking apples.

Prepare the Day Before: Amy's famous carrot salad. One way you can tell a dish is a real show stopper: The cook has gotten so tired of writing out the recipe that it has been mimeographed. My friend Amy hands this one out on printed cards.

Peel the carrots and slice them into disks. Cook in boiling water until just tender. (*Caution!* Do *not* overcook.) Put the carrots into a bowl. Slice the onions into thin rings and add them to the bowl. Cut one green pepper into strips and add that. Then add the can of tomato soup, undiluted, three quarters of a cup of cider vinegar, half a cup of peanut oil, a teaspoon of Worcestershire sauce, a teaspoon of mustard, half a teaspoon of salt. The recipe calls for three quarters of a cup of sugar, but I think that can be cut back to half a cup or less. Mix well and refrigerate.

Prepare Anytime: The applesauce. Cut the cores from six baking apples. Cut the apples into chunks and put them into a covered saucepan with a cup of water. Simmer over low heat until cooked through. Run through the blender and add sugar to taste. Just before serving, add a dash of cinnamon.

3 PM: One of the problems with making your own piecrust: It should be made in advance, then put back into the refrigerator for a couple of hours.

Put two cups of pastry flour into a bowl and mix in one teaspoon of salt. Mix together one third cup of butter and one third cup of lard. Keep some ice water off to the side.

Good cooks tell me the secret of making a perfect piecrust is to work rapidly in mixing together the flour and shortening. The recommended tools: one knife in each hand. Cut the shortening into the flour and keep doing this until it is all mixed together and has the appearance of rough cornmeal.

Sprinkle six tablespoons of the ice water over the mixture and mix that in quickly, using a fork. When it all hangs together, forming a large ball, you've done enough. Wrap it in metal foil and keep it in the refrigerator for a couple of hours.

At this point, you may want to sneak a couple of frozen pieshells from the freezer to thaw—just in case.

5:30 PM: Have two 9-inch pie pans ready. Remove the dough from the refrigerator and cut it into two equal balls. Using a rolling pin (*Danger!* Dust both the rolling pin and the table with flour), roll out the balls of dough. Work from the center out, attempting to create a flat circle about two inches wider than the pan. Put these into the pans and cut away the extra dough from the pan rims. Put the dough back into the refrigerator while you prepare the rest of the quiche.

Fry the bacon in a large pan over medium heat. The bacon should be cooked through but not crisp. Break it into small pieces and set to one side.

Beat three eggs lightly and mix in the light cream, a teaspoon of salt, and the cheese, either grated or cut into small cubes. Preheat the oven to 450 degrees.

6 PM: Remove the piecrusts from the refrigerator. (*Caution!* It's not too late to switch over to the frozen crusts—but in a minute it will be.)

Add the bacon bits to the crust. Then pour in the egg-and-cheese mixture. Pop it into the 450-degree oven for ten minutes, then lower the temperature to 350 degrees. Bake for an additional twenty minutes or until the top is brown. To test for doneness, insert a knife blade. It should come out clean, or fairly clean.

6:20 PM: Cut the tomatoes in half and put the halves on a cookie sheet. Sprinkle with oregano, garlic salt, and a few drops of olive oil. Put the tomatoes under the broiler for just a few minutes and serve piping hot.

MENU 41

Baked Ham
Five-Day Spinach
Potatoes Anna
Flaming Bananas

The meals we serve for our most festive occasions—the turkey at Thanksgiving, the steak on the Fourth, the ham at Easter—are so simple to prepare, so unchallenging, that many cooks would just as soon sit out a holiday season.

Nothing is easier than cooking a non-holiday ham. Oh, I suppose you could buy an uncooked ham and cut away the mold and scrub it with baking soda and allow it to soak in a bathtub for a few days, but there's no reason not to buy a smoked or ready-to-eat ham. All you do then is heat it up, smear on a sauce, heat it some more, and cut it in very thin slices.

Since today's meal is built around such a simple theme, we'll make the rest of it a little more complicated. The Five-Day Spinach, for example, refers not to the fact that the spinach ripens in five days or that it can be eaten over five days, but that it takes five days to cook. That's not so bad. To make a proper Potatoes Anna can take a lifetime.

The Staples: Make sure that these are all on hand: salt, pepper, mustard, beer, rum, whole cloves.

The Shopping List: One ham (twelve to fourteen pounds, precooked or smoked), three pounds potatoes, one and a half pounds butter, two pounds fresh spinach (*very* fresh, if possible), five large bananas, one lemon, brown sugar.

Prepare in Advance: The spinach. Today's recipe for spinach was discovered by the famed food writer Brillat-Savarin, who extracted it from a village priest famous for his spinach. Since I have known only one person who followed this recipe to the letter, I will offer a shorter version as well. (Significantly enough, the one person who went to the trouble received such compliments that she now serves it at *every* dinner party.)

The First Day: Rinse the fresh spinach carefully, removing all traces of sand. Using a heavy but small flameproof casserole pot, melt a stick of butter over low heat. Add the rinsed spinach and cook slowly for half an hour, allowing the butter and the spinach to blend together. Turn off the heat, allow the pot to cool, and put it in the refrigerator.

The Second Day: Put the pan back over very low heat, add half a stick of butter to the spinach, and cook for fifteen minutes; remove from the heat and refrigerate.

The Third Day: Repeat. According to Brillat-Savarin, you must be careful here: "There will be an exceedingly tempting aroma. Do not be tempted."

The Fourth Day: Repeat the process again. ("The spinach will be giving an almost irresistible aroma. Resist.")

The Fifth Day: For the last time repeat the process and cook it over low heat until the butter is fully absorbed by the spinach. And today you don't resist.

A Shortcut: Cook the spinach in half a stick of butter for ten to twelve minutes, or until tender.

3:30 PM (or earlier, for a smoked ham): Allow about fifteen minutes a pound for heating up a ready-to-eat ham, about twenty-five minutes a pound for a smoked ham. Set the oven temperature for 325 degrees. Put in the ham. That's it, for a while.

5 PM: The Potatoes Anna. Peel the potatoes and slice them very thin. Put them into a bowl of ice water. Butter the inside of a medium-sized casserole pot and add a couple of layers of the sliced potatoes. Add dots of butter—perhaps a quarter stick—over the layer of potatoes and a scattering of salt and freshly ground pepper. Now add more potatoes. After every few layers of potatoes, add butter, salt, and pepper, until the potatoes are all in the casserole. Some cooks also add greated onions and Parmesan cheese, but that can wait for another time.

If you have a second oven, cook the potatoes at 400 degrees for approximately an hour. If not, you'll have to cook them in the oven with ham and allow at least an hour and a quarter, probably longer. The potatoes are done when they are brown and crisp on the outside and steaming hot on the inside.

The proper way to serve Potatoes Anna is to turn the pot upside down, forming a brown-surfaced mound of potatoes. (*Danger!* This first time, let's just spoon it directly from the casserole.)

5:45 PM: Oh, yes, the ham. Remove the ham from the oven. If the ham had a rind, cut away the skin and much of the fat. Using a sharp knife, crisscross the surface of the ham with lines. Insert whole cloves—three dozen of them—at the intersections of the cut lines.

Now mix together a cup of brown sugar and three or four tablespoons of mustard. Add just enough of the beer to make this a paste. Smear the paste over the surface of the ham and return it to the oven. Repeat this two or three more times during the baking time.

6:30 PM: The ham, the potatoes, and the spinach should all be done and piping hot. As you remove the food from the oven, turn the heat up to 425 degrees.

Put half a stick of butter into a heatproof dish and melt it in the oven. (Incidentally, it strikes me that this is not a meal for anyone trying to cut down on butter.) Slice the bananas thickly. When the butter is melted, add the sliced bananas and let stand on the counter. Twelve minutes before the end of dinner, interrupt your repast to sprinkle the bananas with the juice of one lemon and dusting of brown sugar and return to the oven for three or four minutes. Finally, add one third cup of rum, strike a match, and serve them alight.

MENU 42

Fillet of Sole
Potatoes O'Brien
Broccoli with Almonds
Fruit Salad

I grew up beside the waters of Puget Sound, and every day before school hours, after school hours, and sometimes during school hours, I could be found beside a river or a bay with a fishing rod in my hands. By the time I was twelve, I knew everything you need to know about cooking fish. The important thing was to catch your fish—say half a dozen trout or a salmon—early in the day. Then, that same day, you dotted the fish with butter, put it under a broiler for a very short time, and served.

I have since learned that this is not the way things go in real life. In real life we buy fish of uncertain origin and inderterminate age, as often as not frozen, and we try to compensate with a sauce.

A good fish sauce—and that is the challenge of today's meal—has always been a problem. Back in the early 1800s, novelist Thomas Love Peacock wrote this lament: "The science of fish sauce . . . is by no means brought to perfection; a fine field of discovery still lies open in that line. . . . I can taste in my mind's palate a combination which, if I could give it a reality, I would christen with the name of my college, and hand it down to posterity as a seat of learning indeed."

Today's sauce has been christened with the name of the school that has meant the most to me personally. Tonight it will be Fillet of Sole with Hard-Knocks Sauce.

Shopping Note: If your fish store doesn't have sole, don't fret. Settle for flounder. That's usually what you get when you order sole in restaurants, anyway. Your most important concern is freshness; the fish should have a springy quality and no pronounced fishy smell.

The Staples: Make sure that these are all on hand: eggs, salt, pepper, parsley, paprika, cream, dry white wine, grenadine syrup.

The Shopping List: Fillets of sole or flounder (three pounds will do for six people), butter, grated Parmesan cheese, eggs, two onions, six medium-sized potatoes, one green pepper, one bunch broccoli, slivered toasted almonds (a quarter pound), one lemon, selection of fruits in season.

Prepare Anytime: The fruit salad. Peel the fruits, chop them, add a few dashes of grenadine syrup, mix well, and refrigerate until used.

5 PM: Potatoes O'Brien is one of the best things that can happen to leftover potatoes. Assuming, however, that you don't have leftover potatoes on hand, you'll begin by manufacturing some.

Boil unpeeled potatoes in a pot of water on medium-high heat until a fork passes easily into them. Twenty minutes should do the job. Then remove them from the heat and drain away the water.

As the potatoes are boiling, melt half a stick of butter in a large frying pan over medium heat. Peel one of the onions, cut it into small pieces, and add to the frying pan. Remove the seeds from the green pepper, cut it into small squares, and add that. Fry together for five or six minutes, then remove from the heat and set to one side.

5:30 PM: Now the broccoli. Rinse the broccoli and cut away the tough portions of the stems. Cut the rest of the stems into small chunks and cook in boiling water. After approximately five minutes, add the rest of the broccoli and cook until just tender.

As the broccoli is cooking, melt one fourth stick of butter in a saucepan, then add the almonds, the juice of half a lemon, and salt and pepper to taste. When the broccoli is cooked through, drain away the water and add the broccoli to the almond mixture. Set to one side.

5:50 PM: Peel the skins from the cooked potatoes and cut the potatoes into small cubes. Add the cubes to the large frying pan with the onions and peppers, stir together, add salt and pepper to taste, and set to one side away from heat.

6 PM: The decks are now clear for the hardest part of the meal, the Fillet of Sole and the Hard-Knocks Sauce.

Put a cup of dry white wine—vermouth is ideal—into a large frying pan and add half an onion, chopped very fine. As this comes to a boil over medium-high heat, add a large pinch of minced parsley and lower the heat.

6:15 PM: Start the potatoes cooking over medium heat and add butter, if needed. Stir occasionally. Warm the broccoli mixture over medium-low heat. Start some water boiling in the bottom portion of a double boiler.

Back to the fish. Add the fish fillets to the simmering wine and poach them gently for a few minutes, until you can flake the fish with a fork. Transport the fish fillets (careful, careful!) to a buttered baking dish.

Set the wine-fish broth cooking over high heat until it has boiled down to about a third of a cup.

Now lower the heat under the double boiler—the water should be hot, not boiling. Melt a stick of butter and add the remaining fish-wine broth. Now add the yolks of four eggs and stir until the sauce thickens. Add two tablespoons of cream, mix, and pour the sauce over the poached fish fillets. Add a generous scattering of Parmesan cheese, a few dashes of paprika, and put the fish under the broiler until the sauce just starts to brown.

MENU 43

Dana's Chicken
Vegetable Medley
Buttermilk Biscuits
Strawberry Sundae

In some families, recipes become heirlooms. They are closely guarded and passed along to each new generation as it comes of age. Before being given the recipe, the heir is often sworn to secrecy, vowing never to reveal the recipe to outsiders.

Dana's Chicken happens to be one of those treasured family recipes. When my niece Dana passed it along to me, I was, of course, pledged to eternal secrecy. I asked if that meant I couldn't print it in this book. Her shattering decision: "Oh, I guess that would be all right."

So be it. Tonight's main dish is easy to make and delicate to the palate, all in all one of the nicest things that can happen to chicken. You will note that our starting point is "boned chicken breasts." As you may or may not know, the boning of a chicken breast, in amateur hands, can be a thoroughly messy affair. The ancient family recipe explains the easiest way to solve this problem. Here's what you do: When ordering the chicken breasts tell your butcher, "Oh, yes, and please remove the bones."

The Staples: Make sure that these are all on hand: salt, pepper, butter, dry white wine (preferably vermouth), flour, baking powder, baking soda.

The Shopping List: Boned chicken breasts (three pounds), one small can beef bouillon, one small container of heavy cream, one lemon, chives, onions (three medium), one package frozen peas, two carrots, one green pepper, five small turnips, six medium potatoes, one pound string beans, one pound asparagus (fresh, if available), buttermilk, one quart vanilla ice cream, one package frozen strawberries.

The vegetable medley requires two hours of very slow cooking, so we'll get that out of the way first. The only test tonight comes in the final moments when a certain scheduling genius is required to get everything to the table at once.

4:15 PM: We'll be using a heavy pot with a tight-fitting cover for the mixed vegetables. Begin by melting a stick of butter over medium heat. As the butter is melting, slice the onions into thin slices and allow them to cook in the butter until they are translucent. As the onions are cooking, cut the tips from the string beans, slice them lengthwise, and add them to the pot. Peel the carrots, the turnips, and the potatoes; cut them into small cubes and add them. Cut the seeds from the green pepper, slice it in thin strips, and add. Add the peas and, finally, the asparagus. Put the heat on low and simmer the vegetables in the covered pot. From time to time, shake the pot gently. (*Caution!* Don't stir the vegetables too frequently or you will find yourself with a pot of baby food.)

5:15 PM: Remove the strawberries from the freezer and allow them to thaw.

5:45 PM: Now the biscuits. It is possible to make simple and successful biscuits from a mix. In fact, I'd recommend that if you can find any without preservatives or additives. Put two cups of sifted flour into a mixing bowl. Add a teaspoon of salt, two teaspoons of baking powder, and one half teaspoon of baking soda. Now add five tablespoons of butter and, holding a knife in each hand, cut in the butter until it is evenly mixed. Add three fourths cup of buttermilk and stir this in with a fork.

Scatter some flour on your work surface and knead the dough with your hands for less than a minute. Flatten the dough against the table until it is about half an inch thick—you can use either your hands or a rolling pin. Now, using a cookie cutter or a juice glass, cut small circles of the dough and put them onto a buttered baking sheet.

6 PM: Preheat the oven to 425 degrees. Since time will be of the essence, carefully assemble all the ingredients that will go into the chicken dish—the chicken, bouillon, wine, lemon, salt, pepper, butter, cream, and chopped chives.

Use a heavy flameproof casserole pot for this dish. Place the pot over medium heat and melt half a stick of butter. When the butter has melted, add the chicken breasts and squeeze half a lemon over them. Add salt and pepper. Now cover the casserole and put it into the hot oven. The chicken breasts should be cooked through in seven or eight minutes; cut into one to be sure.

6:20 PM: As you remove the chicken from the oven, raise the temperature to 450 degrees. Slide in the tray of biscuits; they should be done in ten minutes.

Remove the chicken breasts from the casserole and keep them warm while you make the cream sauce. Put the casserole pot over medium-high heat and add a fourth of a small can of bouillon. Add about the same amount of wine, then boil until the sauce becomes thick, scraping up and mixing in any of the juices that cling to the sides of the pot. Add the heavy cream and boil again until the sauce again turns thick. Pour the sauce over the chicken breasts and top with the chopped chives.

6:30 PM: Quick, now. The biscuits brown from the oven, the vegetables, the chicken—to be followed by ice cream and strawberries.

And one final word. I'd appreciate it personally if you'd keep this one a secret.

MENU 44

The Omelet

===

Most of the dinners we've done have required more time than skill; tonight's will be different. Tonight you will imagine that you're fresh out of time, that the little hand is on the six and the big hand is on the twelve and the natives are getting restless. What do you do?

Almost every cook develops an eleventh-hour special, a saver. Where some would head for the pantry and start opening cans, I'd go to the refrigerator and start opening eggs.

Few dishes have the versatility—or speed—of an omelet. It makes for an impressive breakfast, a first-rate lunch, an easy dinner, and—with the proper additions—a fine dessert. And here's the beauty part: Once you get the hang of it, you can make an omelet in a minute, give or take a few ticks.

Learning how to make an omelet, however, may require somewhat longer than a minute. But there's no need to explain or apologize for those first failed omelets; as you serve them, you simply say, "Here are your scrambled eggs."

The Staples: Make sure that these are all on hand: salt, pepper, butter, Tabasco sauce, and lotsa eggs.

The Other Ingredients: For an omelette *aux fines herbes,* any mixture of the following: parsley, chives, tarragon, watercress, thyme, shallots, garlic. For a cheese omelet: cheese (Swiss or cheddar and Parmesan, grated). For a Western omelet: onion, green pepper, tomato, bacon or ham (a quarter pound). For a dessert omelet: confectioners' sugar, vanilla, jam or jelly.

Special Equipment Note: An omelet is best made in an omelet pan, and the best omelet pans are of heavy cast aluminum with gently sloping edges. Purists will use their omelet pans for nothing else and, furthermore, feel they should never use soap or water on the pan but just wipe it clean with a paper towel after each use. If you do not have an omelet pan in the house, go out and buy one immediately. If you decide to use a standard frying pan, our usual money-back guarantee doesn't hold. Optional but desirable: a narrow spatula.

All our omelets begin the same way except for the dessert omelet. Since the time required is less than a minute, we'll abandon our usual time schedule. And since so little time is required, we'll be making individual two-egg omelets instead of larger ones.

Step 1. Using either a wire whisk or a fork, beat the two eggs briskly in a small bowl. Add two teaspoons of water, a pinch of salt, and a dash of Tabasco sauce.

Step 2. Put the omelet pan over medium heat and wait until it is hot. Test the temperature by allowing a few drops of water to fall onto the pan; when the water bounces like tiny balls and then vanishes, the pan is hot enough.

Step 3. Add a large chunk of butter—between one and two tablespoons—to the hot pan. Give it just a few seconds to melt, then add the egg mixture all at once.

Step 4. It'll be two hands for beginners. In your right hand hold a spatula; in your left hand, the pan. As the eggs begin to set, lift up the edges with the spatula and allow the loose liquid egg to flow into the gap.

Step 5. As the eggs set, shake the pan gently with your left hand, allowing the omelet to slide over the surface of the pan. The eggs will become harder on the outside while remaining creamy inside.

Step 6. Now add the proper filling, spreading it over the half of the omelet that's nearest you.

Step 7. As soon as the filling is in, fold half the omelet over onto the half that has the filling. Now, holding the plate in your left hand and the pan in your right hand, bring the plate up to the pan and allow the omelet to roll gently onto the plate.

Step 8. Repeat steps one through seven.

Now for the most popular omelet fillings. The following should be enough for four or five omelets.

OMELETTE AUX FINES HERBES

Before beginning, mince small handfuls of parsley, chives, tarragon, watercress, thyme, and shallots or garlic—depending on which you've been able to assemble. The herbs can be mixed in with either the eggs or the melted butter.

WESTERN OMELET

Chop up one green pepper, one onion, one tomato, and a quarter pound of bacon or ham. Sauté this until it's done, perhaps twenty minutes. In cooking a Western omelet, I like to use the standard roadside diner technique, mixing a handful of this in with each batch of eggs before making the omelet.

CHEESE OMELET

Before cooking the eggs, set aside six tablespoons of grated cheese—either Swiss or cheddar—and two tablespoons of Parmesan. Just after the eggs set, add the cheese and fold over the omelet. Cook the omelet a few extra seconds to melt the cheese.

DESSERT OMELET

This time we do without the salt, the pepper, or the Tabasco sauce. Instead, for *each* omelet, add a small handful of confectioners' sugar and a half teaspoon of vanilla to the beaten eggs. Just before folding over the omelet, add a large spoonful of your favorite jam or jelly and then a final dusting of sugar.

MENU 45

Vitello Tonnato
Rice Pilaf
Carrots and Scallions
Fruit in Season

I've always liked the unlikely combinations. The old Laurel and Hardy syndrome. I still recall the moment in third grade when my closest friend invited me to sample his peanut butter and mayonnaise sandwich. Peanut butter and *what*? I took a tentative taste. Hmmmm . . . not bad at all. Another taste . . . well, not as bad as it *might* be.

A more recent example. I was in a world-famous Mexican restaurant. The menu was filled with these incongruous combinations. Aha . . . chocolate-covered turkey. It sounded singularly unpromising and looked no better, as though someone had melted a box of bonbons over half a turkey. Well, you can imagine my surprise, on finally digging into it, to discover that what you saw was what you got, one of the most thoroughly repugnant concoctions conjured up in this hemisphere.

Today, another of those unlikely pairings. But this one is an unqualified winner. It's known as Vitello Tonnato. The reason I do not use the English translation: Who would want to eat something called Veal with Tuna Fish Sauce?

The Staples: Make sure that these are all on hand: salt, pepper, peppercorns, bay leaves, olive oil, eggs, garlic, butter.

The Shopping List: Boneless leg of veal (approximately three pounds, tied by butcher), one small can of anchovies, one bottle dry white wine, one small bottle capers, canned chicken consommé (two cups), canned white-meat tuna (approximately six ounces), heavy cream (small container), long-grain white rice, two onions, carrots (two pounds), three lemons, one bunch scallions, celery, parsley, fruit in season.

Although Vitello Tonnato is a summertime favorite, don't let the season scare you off. In fact, there are as many ways to prepare this as there are restaurants in Italy: It can be served cold or hot; the meat can be boiled or baked; the sauce invites experimentation. We'll try one of the easier ways to cook the dish. It takes somewhat longer—forty-eight hours in all—but leaves little to chance.

Prepare Two Days in Advance: The marinade for the meat. Using a large pan, heat four tablespoons of olive oil over medium heat. Add an onion, cut into small pieces; two stalks of celery, including some of the leaves, chopped fine; and three carrots, peeled and chopped. Cook these until the onion becomes tender. Add half the bottle of white wine and bring to a boil. As the liquid is coming to a boil, add three bay leaves, ten peppercorns, several sprigs of parsley, and a large pinch of salt. Allow this to boil for ten or fifteen minutes. Then, as you add the piece of veal, turn the heat off.

When the liquid has cooled sufficiently, refrigerate, allowing the meat to marinate overnight in the wine broth. Occasionally turn the piece of meat over.

Prepare One Day in Advance: The meat. Preheat the oven to 375 degrees. Remove the meat from the marinade and put it into a roasting pan that has been greased with butter. Put the roasting pan into the oven for just one hour. Occasionally baste the meat with some of the marinade while it is roasting.

Later, as the meat is cooling, make the sauce. The sauce should be about the same consistency as cream. It will be easiest to make if all the ingredients are at room temperature.

Put two egg yolks into the blender. Add one cup of olive oil, the tuna fish, drained of all oil, the juice of two lemons, and the anchovies. Turn on the blender and mix until all this forms a heavy, smooth sauce. Now add enough heavy cream to thin it out. Put a small amount of the sauce along the bottom of a shallow platter.

When the meat has cooled, cut it into thin slices and arrange it across the platter. Cover with the remainder of the sauce, making sure that each piece of meat is thoroughly coated. Cover with clear plastic wrap and store in the refrigerator until ready to serve.

5:15 PM: The Rice Pilaf. Using a small pan, melt half a stick of butter over medium heat. Add one onion, chopped fine, two cloves of garlic, minced, a pinch of salt, and some pepper.

When the onion is tender, add a cup of the long-grain rice and allow it to heat for a couple of minutes. Then, add the chicken consommé and bring it to a quick boil. Turn the heat down to low, cover the pot, and allow the rice to cook for just twenty-five minutes. Then turn off the heat.

Now is a good moment to remove the meat from the refrigerator and allow it to come to room temperature.

6 PM: Peel and slice the rest of the carrots. Melt half a stick of butter in a large frying pan over medium heat. Add the sliced carrots, the scallions—whites and some of the greens—chopped fine, some salt, some pepper, and a squeeze of lemon juice. Cook over medium-low heat until the carrots are tender.

6:30 PM: Remove the meat slices from the platter, arrange them on a serving dish, and drape the sauce over them. Garnish with a small handful of capers, sprigs of parsley, and some lemon sections.

MENU 46

Moo Goo Gai Pan
Shabu Shabu
Stir-Fried Green Beans

Lin Yutang once wrote that Chinese cooking skills are a direct result of economic necessity: "We eat all the edible things of this earth. We eat crabs by preference and bark by necessity. . . . We are too overpopulated and famine is too common for us not to eat everything we can lay our hands on."

When you are forced to eat everything you can lay your hands on, bark not excluded, you pretty much have to know what you're doing. What we'll be doing tonight is choosing among three more-or-less Oriental dishes.

Our first dish is Moo Goo Gai Pan, and my feeling is that it is about as authentically Chinese as Charlie Chan's No. 1 son. The next dish, Shabu Shabu, is an authentic Japanese recipe, simple to prepare and surprisingly good.

And then we'll take a look at a way of cooking that originated in the Orient and has become familiar to health food addicts everywhere—stir-fried vegetables.

The Staples: Make sure that these are all on hand: rice, Japanese soy sauce, peanut or corn oil.

Shopping List for Moo Goo Gai Pan: Boned chicken breasts (about one and a half pounds), white wine, one bunch celery, one large onion, one green pepper, one box frozen snow peas, one can water chestnuts, one fourth pound mushrooms.

Shopping List for Shabu Shabu: Beef (one and a half pounds, sliced extremely thin), chicken broth (two cups), two lemons, a selection of radishes, spinach, carrots, mushrooms, scallions, Chinese cabbage. And, from a health food store or Oriental specialty shop: two bean curd cakes, Oriental cellophane noodles, and a seaweed flavoring agent called kombu.

Shopping List for Stir-Fried Green Beans: One pound green beans and one can water chestnuts.

MOO GOO GAI PAN

Sometime in Advance: Cut the chicken breasts into half-inch cubes and soak in enough white wine to cover them.

Prepare Slightly in Advance: The rice. Follow the directions on the box so that the rice will be completed at 6:30 PM. Remove the snow peas from the freezer and allow them to thaw.

6 PM: Now for the rest of the meal. Much of the effort that goes into any Oriental food is preparation, which most often takes the form of slicing and dicing.

Begin by rinsing the stalks of celery and slicing them thin. Peel the onion and cut that in paper-thin slices. Dice the green pepper. Drain the liquid from the water chestnuts and slice them. Remove the tips from the stems, then slice the mushrooms. Have the defrosted pea pods at hand.

Use a wok if possible, a large frying pan if no wok is available. Place the pan over medium-high heat for several moments, then add a spash—a three-tablespoon splash—of oil.

Remove the chicken pieces from the wine marinade and stir them into the hot oil. Stir with a wooden spoon for a couple of minutes, then add the celery, the onion, the green pepper, and the pea pods. Keep stirring for a few minutes more as the chicken pieces cook through—they'll be white—and then add the water chesnuts and the mushrooms. After a few more minutes, add three or four tablespoons of soy sauce and the wine marinade. Cook for about five minutes more and serve over rice.

SHABU SHABU

As before, we begin by cooking the rice so that it will be ready at 6:30. And then, once again, we go right into the slicing and dicing: the beef, the Chinese cabbage, the spinach, the scallions, the mushrooms, and the peeled carrots, cut into matchstick shapes.

Mix together the chicken broth and an equal amount of water and bring to a boil over medium heat. Then add portions of the vegetables—a handful of the shredded cabbage, the spinach, the carrots, the scallions, the mushrooms, and the noodles. If you were lucky enough to find a piece of kombu, add that. Allow this to cook for a few minutes and then add a share of the meat. The meat should boil for just a few minutes.

Serve this mixture, removed from the liquid, over rice. In a side dish, serve a sauce consisting of half soy sauce, half lemon juice and grated radish. In a second side dish, put the sliced bean curds doused in soy sauce and mixed with chopped scallions. The side dishes are spooned onto the main dish according to taste.

STIR-FRIED GREEN BEANS

Cut away the tips of the green beans and cut them into pieces. Drain the water chestnuts and slice them. Put the wok over high heat and add a three-tablespoon splash of oil. When hot, add the green beans. Stir. After a couple of minutes, add the water chestnuts. Cook for two or three minutes more, stirring constantly. Add one third cup of water. Cover the vegetables, allow them to steam for three or four minutes, and serve at once.

MENU 47

Cheese Crepes or
Stuffed Ham Crepes or
Crepes Suzette

Tonight we'll be doing a scene from a thousand Hollywood movies, the scene that always symbolized The Good Life . . . Sophisitication . . . Class. The camera pans around a large room—low-cut gowns, wine bottles in silver buckets, a small string orchestra, tuxedos. Now the close-up—the white linen tablecloth, the crystal goblets, a waiter's hand touching a match to a pan, setting off a small explosion, and the whispering of one knowledgeable moviegoer to another: "Crepes Suzette!"

That was class, vintage 1948. But in France today the street-corner crepes stand is as common a sight as the hot dog stand in this country. Ah, it's the story of our times— from class to junk food in less than a generation.

Why the international popularity of the crepe? Because it's an all-purpose food, welcome as an appetizer, a main dish, or a dessert.

It's as versatile as an omelet, easier to make, and can be made in advance and reheated.

We'll try three different crepes. Incidentally, it might be a good idea *not* to have them all on a single evening.

Ingredients for the Basic Crepe: Three eggs, one and a half cups flour, one cup milk, one half cup water, two tablespoons melted butter, dash of salt, pinch of sugar.

Ingredients for Cheese Crepes: Grated Parmesan cheese (three quarters of a cup), parsley, thyme.

Ingredients for Ham Crepes: Boneless cooked ham (one pound), beef bouillon (one and a quarter cups), one onion, mushrooms (one half pound), butter, sherry, flour.

Ingredients for Crepes Suzette: Sugar cubes, butter, vanilla, two oranges, Grand Marnier, cognac.

THE BASIC CREPE

The batter for the crepes should be made at least an hour or two before the actual cooking.

We'll be using an electric mixer at medium-low speed. Begin by beating the eggs until they are well blended. Then add about half the flour and mix that in well. Now add the rest of the flour, the salt, and the sugar. Then beat in the milk, a little bit at a time, then the water, and then the melted butter. The batter should have the consistency of heavy cream.

If there's a crepe pan on the premises, by all means use that. Otherwise a 6-inch frying pan should do nicely. Use a small ladle—a couple of tablespoons of batter should make one crepe.

Put a pat of butter into a hot pan over medium heat and, as soon as it's melted, add the batter and tilt the pan to allow it to spread evenly over the entire surface.

Stay on your toes now. To make a proper crepe requires about a minute on the first side, half that time for the second side. Peeking is allowed; the first side should be a nice even pale brown.

If you're making the crepes ahead of time, place a piece of waxed paper between them as you stack them. Butter the pan as it dries out.

THE APPETIZER: CHEESE CREPES

To make the cheese crepe, you simply add a few ingredients before cooking. Before adding the milk to the batter, add the grated cheese, a small handful of ground parsley, and a pinch of thyme. Cook as you would cook any crepe and serve hot with butter or melted cheese.

THE MAIN DISH: HAM CREPES

Chop the onion and the mushrooms and cut the ham into small cubes. Heat half a stick of butter in a skillet over medium heat and cook the chopped onion until soft. Then add the ham and the mushrooms and a splash of sherry and cook together for a few minutes.

Now add two tablespoons of flour and a small splash of beef bouillon. Mix together until smooth and then add the rest of the bouillon and cook until the sauce is thick.

Put some of the sauce into each crepe. Roll the crepes up and arrange them in a baking dish. Drape the rest of the sauce over the crepes and bake in a 350-degree oven for twenty minutes.

THE DESSERT: CREPES SUZETTE

There are many recipes for this dish, most of them extraordinarily complicated. This is one of the less elaborate versions. In making the crepes for this or any other dessert, you can replace some of the water with a few tablespoons of cognac, a dash of vanilla, and a little more sugar.

Once the crepes are made, we'll move on to the sauce. Begin by grating three tablespoons of orange rind and then squeezing the oranges.

Place a large skillet over medium heat. When the pan is hot, add some sugar cubes (about sixteen of the small-sized cubes). As the cubes begin to melt, add one fourth cup of cognac. Light this with a match and allow it to burn for a moment. Then add a stick of butter and, as it melts, stir it in with the sugar.

Add one half cup of orange juice and one half cup of Grand Marnier. As this is cooking, fold each crepe in half, then in quarters, and douse it in the hot mixture. When all the crepes have been done, add one quarter cup of cognac and light it a second time. Skilled chefs will serve the individual crepes in full flame, but my feeling is there's no need to press your luck immediately.

MENU 48

Gosky Patties
Lobster Newburg
Brown Rice
Spinach Provençal
Oatmeal Cookies

Often I am asked what is my "favorite" recipe. My favorite recipe is Edward Lear's recipe for Gosky Patties. It goes this way:

"Take a pig three or four years of age, and tie him by the off hind leg to a post. Place five pounds of currants, three of sugar, two pecks of peas, eighteen roast chestnuts, a candle, and six bushels of turnips within his reach; if he eats these, constantly provide him with more.

"Then procure some cream, some slices of Cheshire cheese, four quires of foolscap paper, and a packet of black pins. Work the whole into a paste, and spread it out to dry on a sheet of clean brown waterproof linen.

"When the paste is prefectly dry, but not before, proceed to beat the pig violently with the handle of a large broom. If he squeals, beat him again.

"Visit the paste and beat the pig alternately for some days, and ascertain if, at the end of that period, the whole is about to turn into Gosky Patties. If it does not then, it never will; and in that case the pig may be let loose, and the whole process may be considered as finished."

Okay, that's my favorite recipe. What follows, on the other hand, is one of my favorite meals.

The Staples: Make sure that these are all on hand: salt, pepper, olive oil, eggs, garlic, brown sugar, vanilla, flour, baking soda, baking powder, brandy, lemon, paprika.

The Shopping List: Lobster (enough for two cups of cooked meat; lobster tails will be easiest), heavy cream, one large onion, fresh spinach (one pound), butter, rolled oats, brown rice.

Prepare in Advance: The Gosky Patties.

Also Prepare in Advance: The oatmeal cookies. You'll be using an electric beater at medium speed. Preheat the oven to 350 degrees. Then mix together a cup of brown sugar and one half cup of soft butter. In a second bowl, beat together one egg, a dash of vanilla, and one tablespoon of heavy cream. Mix the contents of the two bowls together.

Now mix together one cup of flour, one half teaspoon of baking soda, and one half teaspoon of baking powder. Add to the batter and mix. Next add one cup of rolled oats.

Beat all these ingredients together until the mixture is smooth. Butter the surface of a cookie sheet and drop a tablespoon of the batter every couple of inches. Bake for twelve minutes, or until the cookies are nicely browned, then remove from the oven.

Also Prepare in Advance: The lobster meat. Whether you use live lobster (*Caution:* if you've purchased live lobster, make sure it *is* live) or frozen lobster tails, the easiest way to prepare the meat is simply to boil it, allow it to cool, and then remove it from the shells. Cut the meat into half-inch chunks and set to one side.

5:30 PM: The rice. Why brown rice instead of white rice? The Lobster Newburg sauce will make the rice all taste the same, and brown rice is much better for you. Ignore the directions on the box and cook it this way: Heat two and a quarter cups of water to a boil and add one cup of dry brown rice. When the water returns to the boil, lower the heat and cover the pot. It should be ready in just forty-five minutes.

6 PM: The spinach. Carefully rinse the sand from the spinach leaves. The easiest way to do this is to dip the leaves into a large pot of cool water; the safest way to do this is three times.

In a large skillet, melt a quarter stick of butter and add a splash of olive oil. Add the large onion, chopped fine, and two cloves of garlic, minced. Allow this to cook until the onion softens, then add the spinach, lower the heat, and cover the skillet. Just before serving, add a squeeze of lemon.

6:15 PM: The Lobster Newburg. You'll be using a double boiler to make the sauce. Separate three eggs and hang on to the yolks. Put them into the top half of the double boiler over hot—but not boiling—water. Add a cup of heavy cream and a pinch of salt and pepper. Stir until the sauce begins to thicken, then remove from the heat.

In a separate saucepan, melt half a stick of butter over medium-low heat and add the chunks of lobster. When the lobster is warmed through, add a healthy splash—oh, one fourth cup—of brandy and touch a match to it. Allow it to flame for a couple of minutes, then mix together the lobster and the sauce and a large pinch of paprika.

Check the rice to make sure the liquid has all cooked away. Check the spinach to make sure it is tender. Serve the Lobster Newburg over the rice and beside the Spinach Provençal.

You will follow this, if everything has worked out satisfactorily, with the Gosky Patties. If not, settle for the oatmeal cookies.

Incidentally, sometimes I am asked what is my second favorite recipe. That is the recipe for Amblongus Pie, also by Edward Lear. It begins in this fashion: "Take four pounds (say four and a half pounds) of fresh Amblonguses, and put them in a small pipkin." And it concludes: "Serve up in a clean dish and throw the whole out of the window as fast as possible."

MENU 49

Paella de Manhattan

Behind every recipe there is a story, and this is no exception. Paella is a Spanish dish, perhaps *the* Spanish dish, and we should not be surprised to learn that the story behind this recipe is fiery, tempestuous, and romantic—a modern love story. And since it is Paella de Manhattan, it will be a love story with a big-city setting.

The story, incidentally, is a true one; it comes from the young man who first gave me the recipe. It seems that our hero had been living in a Manhattan apartment for several years, during which time he realized that young woman in the very next apartment was more than moderately attractive.

For several more years they shared corridors and elevators until finally the young woman knocked on his door, asked to borrow a cup of Cointreau, and, in the process, introduced herself. Several more years passed, and the woman asked her neighbor if he would like to stop by that evening for supper.

He agreed. That night the woman served paella, the very same paella that we'll be making today. Hereafter, our story picks up speed. The young man took a single mouthful and gasped out his pleasure. Halfway through dinner he tendered a serious proposal of marriage. Over coffee and brandy, they set the date just two weeks hence.

Well, the paella was consumed and the marriage was consummated, and they lived happily ever after for about a year and a half (remember, this is a modern New York love story), at which time there were fights, tears, a costly divorce, a bitter custody fight, and the usual alimony and child-support payments.

The moral: Never make the mistake of confusing one dish with another.

The Staples: Make sure that these are all on hand: salt, pepper, garlic, saffron (a must!), tarragon, flour, olive oil, bay leaves, one chicken bouillon cube.

The Shopping List: (Brace yourself!) As much of the following as you can locate: one chicken (three to four pounds, cut into finger pieces), sausage (one half pound Spanish chorizo or hot pepperoni), clams (one pound) and/or mussels (one pound), mushrooms (one pound), large shrimps (one pound), onions (one pound), three sweet red peppers, frozen peas (one box), pimientos (one small jar), green olives (one dozen, without pits), parsley, white rice, two cans chicken bouillon, white wine.

Since so many different things have to be cooked so many different ways, a schedule would be hopelessly optimistic. Allow between two and three hours and at least one practice session.

We'll be taking the coward's way out tonight. The true Spaniard would cook the rice and the rest of this in a single pot. And occasionally the true Spaniard would come up with a glutinous mess. We'll be cooking the ingredients separately and joining them together at the last moment.

We'll begin by preparing everything we're going to need. Scrub the clams and mussels with a heavy brush, then scrub them again; the one ingredient that doesn't go well in a paella is sand.

Then peel the onions and chop them fine. Chop the olives and pimientos. Separate the mushroom stems and caps. Chop the red peppers. Peel and clean the shrimps. Allow the peas to thaw.

Using a heavy large skillet over medium heat, warm up a generous splash of olive oil and add the onions, peppers, and two cloves of garlic, minced. As the onions begin to turn translucent, add the mushrooms and cook for five minutes more. Put all these ingredients into one bowl.

Add another splash of oil to the skillet and, while it is heating up, coat the chicken pieces with flour. Put a cup of flour into a brown paper bag, along with a generous amount of salt and pepper, then add the chicken pieces and shake vigorously. Fry the chicken pieces until they are cooked through, then put them into another bowl.

Meanwhile, back at the skillet, add another splash of olive oil and another garlic clove, minced. Then add the sliced sausage and the peeled shrimps. Cook until the sausage is well browned and place this in still another bowl.

Back to the skillet. Add another splash of olive oil. And here we'll add a cup of white wine, two bay leaves, the bouillon cube, a handful of minced parsley, and a pinch of tarragon. Then add the clams and/or mussels, both of which have been scrubbed clean. Cover the pot and steam just until the clams and/or mussels open up. If they don't open, discard them. Set the shellfish to one side and add the peas to the broth for just two or three minutes. Remove the peas and hold them aside.

Cook two cups of dry rice according to the directions on

the box. Instead of water, use a mixture of the clam-mussel broth and the canned chicken bouillon, along with a teaspoon of saffron. When the rice is done, mix in the chopped olives, the pimientos, and the peas.

From now on, it's a matter of achieving the proper visual effect. Put the rice into a heavy casserole and add everything except the shellfish. Mix *very lightly* with the fork, trying not to unfluff the rice. Finally, scatter the clams and/or mussels over the top of the paella and add a dusting of minced parsley.

Put the casserole into a 325-degree oven and serve hot, in about fifteen minutes.

MENU 50

Oysters Rockefeller
New Potatoes
Sautéed Mushrooms
Devil's Food Cake

I guess it all depends on where you grew up. I look on today's meal as one of those good old-fashioned, down-home
country meals, the kind your Aunt Frances used to make—
that is, if your Aunt Frances happened to live beside an oys-
ter bed.

Which, fortunately, my Aunt Frances did. And she still
serves up her incredible Oysters Rockefeller every couple of
weeks, adding this and subtracting that, sometimes mixing
in a local seaweed and sometimes settling for spinach, always wondering whether it's anything like the dish served
in New Orleans.

Oysters Rockefeller was invented there, at one of the
world's most celebrated restaurants, Antoine's.

However, Antoine's has refused to part with the original
recipe, offering instead what is called "a close facsimile."

There came a time, not too long ago, when we found our-
selves at Antoine's, ordering Oysters Rockefeller. This was

it, the big time, and we felt as awed as any bush-league player finally walking into Yankee Stadium. We took a taste, then another. It was good . . . it was *very* good . . . it was *almost* as good as the Oysters Rockefeller that my Aunt Frances makes.

So what follows is her recipe, and I don't mean a close facsimile thereof.

The Staples: Make sure that these are all on hand: salt, pepper, dry mustard, garlic, granulated sugar, baking soda, two eggs, flour, vanilla, almond extract.

The Shopping List: Oysters (four dozen), butter (one half pound), buttermilk, bacon (one half pound), one onion, one bunch of parsley, two lemons, spinach (one pound), potatoes (three pounds), scallions or chives, large mushrooms (one pound), bread crumbs, cocoa.

Prepare in Advance: The devil's food cake. Another family note. The recipe that has caused the most favorable comment was my grandmother's whole wheat bread, made with bacon fat. This is her devil's food cake, also made with bacon fat, equally good.

Preheat the oven to 325 degrees. You'll begin by browning the bacon for the Oysters Rockefeller, setting the bacon aside, and using half a cup of the bacon fat now.

Using an electric beater on medium speed, cream together the bacon fat and one and a half cups of sugar. Then add two eggs and mix well.

In another bowl, mix together three quarters of a cup of dry cocoa and half a cup of hot water into a smooth paste. Mix the contents of the two bowls, along with one teaspoon of baking soda, half a cup of buttermilk, one and a half cups of flour and a teaspoon of vanilla.

When all the ingredients are smoothly blended, pour into two greased and floured cake tins and bake for half an hour.

While the cake is baking, make the frosting. Mix two thirds cup of hot water, two cups of sugar, and one eighth teaspoon of almond extract. Boil for about two minutes. When it has cooled to lukewarm, beat it with an electric mixer until it's white. Spread it in between the layers and over the cake when the cake has cooled sufficiently.

5:15 PM: The new potatoes. While the water is coming to a boil, peel the potatoes. Cook the potatoes in boiling water for just five minutes. Then put them into a baking dish with a melted stick of butter, a handful of scallions (or chives), chopped fine, and a large pinch of minced parsley. The potatoes will bake in the oven at the same time as the Oysters Rockefeller.

5:30 PM: The Oysters Rockefeller. I'm assuming the oysters are not in the shells. If they are, just smear the rest of the ingredients over them and bake them on the half shell in a very hot oven (475 degrees for fifteen minutes).

Otherwise, try it this way. In a frying pan over medium heat, melt half a stick of butter. Add half an onion, chopped fine, and cook it until it turns translucent. Add the rinsed spinach and cook that for five or six minutes.

The butter-onion-spinach mixture goes into the blender, along with the juice of one lemon, a handful of parsley, and one half teaspoon of dry mustard. Mix it all together.

Cut the oysers into small pieces, drain away the liquid, and put them into the bottom of a shallow baking dish. Cover the oysters with an even layer of the spinach mixture. Top with a layer of bread crumbs and dot the surface with the browned bacon pieces.

Preheat the oven to 425 degrees.

6 PM: Put both oven dishes—potatoes and oysters—into the preheated oven. They should be ready in half an hour.

6:15 PM: Place the large mushroom caps in a frying pan with half a stick of butter over medium heat. Add one garlic clove, minced, and stir occasionally. Cook about ten minutes, then add a large pinch of minced parsley and a generous amount of salt and pepper. Lower the temperature.

6:30 PM: Test the potatoes for doneness. Before serving, add the juice of one lemon, salt, and pepper.

MENU 51

Cheese Soufflé
Green-Bean-and-Tomato Salad
Apricots in Cognac

Ah, we near the end of the road. When we began this experiment just fifty-one menus ago, we had several goals. The first goal here was to offer a simple, easy-to-follow guided tour through my favorite meals. The second goal was to take a spectacularly inexperienced cook—say, a typical husband—and move him in slow, sure steps from spaghetti to Chicken Kiev (coming up next). A third goal, most ambitious of all, was to transform the kitchen into an equal opportunity establishment.

Today's meal may not be the final exam, but it can be a test for any cook. I've tried most of the different soufflé recipes and have managed to demolish a fair share of them; in fact, you're reading the man who put the lie to Julia Child's "Never-Fail Soufflé." Incidentally, be forewarned—nothing fails quite so dramatically as a soufflé. I would as soon serve quicksand to dinner guests as a squashed soufflé.

I've found this particular soufflé to be practically indestructible. All you have to do is take it one step at a time and observe all the little (*Danger!*) signs along the way. Time will be all-important. A perfect soufflé is like a perfect sunset; it has a life expectancy of less than ten minutes. So let's get on with it.

The Staples: Make sure that these are all on hand: salt, pepper, paprika, cayenne pepper, milk, butter, wine vinegar, olive oil, cognac, sugar, flour.

The Shopping List: Large eggs, sharp cheddar cheese (three quarters of a pound), grated Parmesan cheese (four ounces), fresh green beans (one pound), ripe tomatoes (one pound), scallions (one bunch), dried apricots (one box), ice cream (optional).

Prepare at Least Two Days in Advance: The apricots. Nothing could be simpler than this. Mix the box of dried apricots with one-third cup of sugar and enough cognac to give all the apricots a bath. Refrigerate for at least two days and then serve cold, either with or without a scoop of ice cream.

Prepare Earlier in the Day: The salad. Chop off the tips of the green beans, slice them, and then cook them in boiling water for just a few minutes; they should not be soggy. Rinse the tomatoes and cut them into small chunks. Chop up the scallions (the whites and about an inch of the green). Add salt, pepper, half the Parmesan cheese, two tablespoons of wine vinegar, and about four times that much olive oil. Stir the ingredients until all the green beans are coated with the salad dressing, then refrigerate until ready to serve.

5 PM: And now there is nothing to do but the soufflé. The first thing we'll do is get the equipment in order. You'll want an electric beater, a wire whisk, and a variety of bowls and pans. Also soufflé pans—straight-sided ovenproof casserole dishes. You'll be making enough for two medium-sized soufflés.

We'll begin by making the cheese filling. Grate the cheddar cheese and set it to one side. Using either a saucepan over low heat or the top half of a double boiler, melt one stick of butter. (*Caution!* The heat should be low enough that the butter melts without browning.) Just as the butter melts, add one half cup of flour and stir with a wire whisk until it forms a smooth paste.

As the butter is melting, heat two and a half cups of milk in a separate saucepan over high heat. (*Danger!* Don't start any other major projects at this moment. When the milk starts to boil, it will bubble out over the stove in a matter of seconds.)

Just as the milk starts to boil—you'll see the bubbles forming on its surface—take it away from the heat and pour it into the butter sauce. Stir with a whisk until it forms a thick white sauce. Remove from the heat and add a teaspoon of salt, another of paprika, and a healthy dash of cayenne pepper.

Wait a minute ot two, then stir in the grated cheddar cheese until it melts. Give it another couple of minutes to cool, then start adding the egg yolks, one at a time, eight in all. Using an electric mixer, beat after adding each yolk. Save the whites in a separate bowl.

Set the cheese filling to one side and allow it to cool off until it's lukewarm.

5:40 pm: Preheat the oven to 375 degrees.

Now, the egg whites. (*Danger!* First, rinse the electric mixer blades and bowl and dry them thoroughly.) In beating the egg whites, you'll be doing a small tightrope act. They should be stiff enough to stand up in peaks, but not too dry or frothy. When you've got them just so, fold them into the cheese sauce. (*Danger!* Do *not* mix or stir, just fold and turn.) The idea is a simple one: You do not want to lose the airy quality of the egg whites because that's what makes a soufflé what it is.

Butter the bottoms and sides of the soufflé pans—the easiest way to do this is with a piece of paper napkin smeared in soft butter. Dust each pan with half the Parmesan cheese. Now add the soufflé mixture. (*Danger!* Not *all* the way up, just about three quarters of the way up.)

Check it in thirty-five minutes. It should be lightly browned on the outside and still moist on the inside, a piece of transient culinary sculpture guaranteed to generate more than the usual number of oohs and ahhhs. (*Danger!* Allow only two oohs and ahhhs per guest before serving—otherwise they'll be staring at a plate of scrambled eggs.)

MENU 52

Chicken Kiev
Cold Asparagus Vinaigrette
Barley-Mushroom Casserole
Figs in Sour Cream

Graduation day, at last. As I look out over your shining faces, the shining faces of the most promising class in this institution's history, I'm compelled to deliver a few parting remarks.

In the first place, I know it hasn't been easy. You've got every right to feel proud. If you've cooked the fifty-two complete meals, you've mastered the basics of cookery. You've learned, for example, that there are appliances in a kitchen other than the refrigerator. Many of you have learned which switch turns on which burner.

All that separates you from your diploma is one little test. And here it is, the final exam ... Chicken Kiev.

The Staples: Make sure that these are all on hand: salt, pepper, flour, cinnamon, garlic, tarragon, wine vinegar, olive oil, crème de cacao.

The Shopping List: Chicken breasts (three pounds, boned and flattened by your butcher), asparagus (two pounds), pearl barley, figs (one pound, fresh or canned), one small container sour cream, butter, eggs, parsley, scallions, mushrooms (half a pound), celery, vegetable oil (one and a half quarts, for frying), chicken bouillon (three cups), seasoned bread crumbs.

Prepare in Advance: The asparagus. Rinse the asparagus carefully and cut away the tough ends of the stalks. The best way to boil asparagus is to use a tall, covered pot and to stand them upright in two or three inches of boiling water. The time required: approximately fifteen minutes.

As the asparagus is cooking, prepare the vinaigrette sauce. To three fourths cup of olive oil, add one fourth cup of wine vinegar. Then add salt, pepper, two minced garlic cloves, a small handful of chopped scallions, and a large pinch of chopped parsley. Coat the asparagus with the dressing and refrigerate until ready to serve.

Also Prepare in Advance: The barley casserole. Using a large frying pan over medium heat, melt half a stick of butter. Add a large handful of chopped scallions and four stalks of celery, also chopped. Cook until the celery softens, then add the mushrooms, sliced. Cook for four or five minutes more and set the vegetables to one side in a bowl.

Using the same pan and the same amount of butter, cook one and a half cups of pearl barley until it begins to turn brown. Put the barley mixture into a casserole dish. Add the vegetables and a handful of chopped parsley and set to one side.

Also Prepare in Advance: The dessert. If the figs are canned, drain away the syrup. If fresh, peel away the skin

and slice the fruit. Mix the sour cream with three or four tablespoons of crème de cacao. Immerse the figs in the cream
mixture, sprinkle with cinnamon, and refrigerate until
ready to serve.

Also Prepare in Advance: Most of the Chicken Kiev.
Chicken Kiev is a deep-fried chicken cutlet stuffed with
butter and herbs. Much of the difficult work here could
be—and should be—done by your butcher. Ask him to
bone the chicken breasts and flatten them.

Lay the cutlet flat on a piece of waxed paper. Put a small
finger of butter—perhaps a tablespoon—on the broadest
part of the chicken. Add pinches of spices. Measurements
don't have to be exact, but keep the pinches on the small
side—a little minced garlic, a little tarragon, a bit of parsley.
Roll the chicken around the herbs like a blanket and use a
toothpick to hold it all together.

Set up an assembly-line operation of three bowls. In the
first bowl, a cup of flour. In the second, an egg beaten together with the yolks of four other eggs. In the final bowl,
the flavored bread crumbs.

Roll the chicken in the flour, then dip it into the egg mixture. Finally, roll it into the bread crumbs so that it's completely covered. Wrap the cutlets in waxed paper and keep
cold until you cook them.

5:15 PM: Preheat the oven to 350 degrees.

5:30 PM: Add one and a half cups of chicken bouillon to the
barley mixture in a covered casserole and put it into the
oven. In a half hour, remove the barley casserole from the
oven and add the final one and a half cups of chicken bouillon. Leave the cover off and return the dish to the oven.

The barley will be done when all liquid is absorbed (about thirty minutes).

6 PM: Start the vegetable oil heating in either a deep fryer or an electric frying pan—set the temperature for 375 degrees. At 375 degrees, the Chicken Kiev will cook in four to five minutes. It should be a rich brown on the outside, and the butter should be steaming hot on the inside. As the cutlets finish cooking—cut into one to check doneness—allow them to drain on paper towels. They should be cooked as close to serving as possible; the perfect Chicken Kiev will emit a small geyser of melted butter and herbs when you cut into it.

And that should do it, graduates. Thanks for your kind attention and good luck.

INDEX

224